Follow the "nudges" life
and live your
ALIVE!

HRShultz

What Others Are Saying About
Living Your Life Alive

"If you have excuses for why you can't live your best life...*Living Your Life Alive* is the one book you better start reading."

— Mel Robbins, Motivational Speaker and TEDx Sensation with over 4 million views. Bestselling Author of *Stop Saying You're Fine* and *The 5 Second Rule*

"*Living Your Life Alive* is not only a peek into what your life could be like living it fully alive, but it gives you real tools and exercises that will actually take you there. You are worth it! Pick up your copy today."

— Chris Widener, Author of *The Art of Influence*

"Autumn Shields has delivered a powerful book that will transform your life if you let it. She has a great way of making the complex seem simple, and she offers what you want—a way to live your life alive! Pick up your copy today, soar to new heights, and achieve your destiny!"

— Patrick Snow, International Best-Selling Author of *Creating Your Own Destiny* and *The Affluent Entrepreneur*

"Autumn has the whole package. When I heard she was writing this book, I knew instantly that I was going to get it. I wanted to know what secrets she knew that I had yet to figure out. She is beautiful, successful, and carries herself well. I naturally wanted to learn more about how she lives her life. I was drawn in. But then I read the book. Autumn really has it all figured out! She's going to take you places you've never been, and by the time you get to the end of this book, you're going to be motivated to get out there and live your life alive!"

— Nicole Gabriel, Author of *Finding Your Inner Truth* and *Stepping Into Your Becoming*

"Clean and straightforward, the overall feeling of this powerful and dynamic book is one of calm acceptance, encouraging you to stop and think before moving on with your busy and hectic life."

— Susan Friedmann, CSP, International Best-Selling Author of
Riches in Niches: How to Make it BIG in a small Market

"Taking that first step to reclaim your beautiful life from fear can be overwhelming. How do I start? Where do I go? Who can help me? Am I even worthy? These questions may have paralyzed you a thousand times before. But today is different from all those other attempts because with beginning the journey of *Living Your Life Alive* by Autumn Shields, you will have a guide, mentor, and friend who will liberate you to live the life you were born to live."

— Luis De La Fuente, Author of *Life Lessons from the Lantern*

"A sparkling presentation of living life. A positive message of healing and hope."

— Dr. Michael McBride, Founder of Somatic Energies

"If you're not living your life, barely living your life, or living a life of lack and compromise, then this is the book for you! Autumn Shields, an inspirational author whose life purpose has been to lift up, empower, and educate others, uses both her education and (most importantly) her life experiences to show you the way. This book will speak to your soul; and if you let it, it will change your life! You owe it to yourself to read this book."

— Nancy Byrne, Author of *Choices*

"I was deeply touched and inspired by your story and who you are—wow!"

— Grace Purusha, Owner of The Center for Radiant Aliveness

"If you feel that you are existing rather than living, then this is a must-read. Autumn Shields has impressive experience working with people who have extreme challenges in their lives, so she is the perfect person to help you truly to live. *Living Your Life Alive* is a life-changing book."

— Karen Degen, Author of *Heightening Your Happiness*

What Others Are Saying About Autumn Shields

"Autumn is a great example of living your life alive. Kudos to her for her willingness to help others overcome what may be keeping them from fulfilling their own dreams."

— Caren Teves Founder of NO NOTORIETY, dedicated to reducing senseless loss of life caused by acts of mass violence— honoring the life and memory of Alexander C. Teves, The Aurora12, and all those affected by acts of violence.

"I have always encouraged Autumn to write a book. She has more than a story; she has experienced a journey of finding herself as a mother, leader, and business owner. Autumn was able to work through and overcome obstacles most would fall victim to and back down from. Her ability to show grace, love, and support provides Autumn with a unique insight and ability to inspire those around her to dream bigger, learn more, and live out their 'Why.' Autumn's gifts of empathy and compassion give her a true advantage in leadership, because they are where trust is born. Autumn is the first person I have known to discover her 'Why,' and then have the courage to live it."

— Philip Saraff, Optimist and Entrepreneur, ORIS Consulting Group LLC, Law Enforcement—Police Officer for twenty years

"I met Autumn when we were young public servants working together in municipal court as our careers were just starting out. Autumn has always had a positive attitude in both her personal and professional life. Autumn has the ability to connect with people in a profound way. Her desire and excitement to empower others is truly evident in her everyday persona. She provides concise and simple suggestions to help people make positive choices. I have seen firsthand how she has mitigated and improved people's lives. I have also experienced Autumn's advice in my personal life. Her encouragement and her simple suggestions have helped me immensely. I respect her most for her personal courage in life. She has navigated some difficult waters, and after each adversity, she learns and improves from her misfortunes. Sometimes we all lose sight of our happiness, but Autumn has always had a knack for encouraging people to rediscover what really makes them happy. I have seen Autumn's dynamic range of serving others in both a professional and personal setting."

— Luis Martinez, Denver Firefighter for twenty years

A SELF-LEADERSHIP BLUEPRINT TO EXECUTE YOUR INNERMOST PASSIONS

LIVING
YOUR LIFE
ALIVE

LEARNING TO
LISTEN AND
FOLLOW YOUR
INNER NUDGE

AUTUMN SHIELDS

AVIVA
PUBLISHING
New York

To my son, Braxton Makoa Black.
I am so proud of your strength and faith.
I encourage you always to follow your passions,
lead with your heart, forgive, and love deeply.
You deserve the best!

To my readers—you! Thank you for being you.
This book is for you.

ACKNOWLEDGMENTS

To my God: You are my everything. Your love is the answer.

To the reader: Thank you for giving me the honor of sharing this book with you.

So many people have helped me along the way in my education, my career, and my life's work. I would like to thank my family, each friend, client, and business partner for your support, guidance, referrals, and the unique effect you have had on my life.

To my parents, Barry and Nancy Shields: Thank you for your unwavering support. Thank you for modeling entrepreneurship, great business ethics, and stewardship. I love you both and am so grateful.

To my brother and sister-in-law, Andy and Rachel Shields, and to my nephew, Luke: Thank you for being solid in my life and such great examples of servant love.

To my closest girlfriends (you know who you are): Thank you for being able to play small and big roles in my life. Thank you for supporting and encouraging me in living my life alive.

To Jeff Black: Thank you for helping me learn one of my most valuable life lessons and for Braxton.

To Robin Chew: Thank you for offering me the opportunity in network marketing that forever changed the course of my life.

To Sean, Jacob, and Alexa Saraff (my stepchildren): Thank you for sharing your younger years with me.

To the people who were able to guide me legally over the years, I am forever indebted: Jan, Jim, Annie, Andy, and Jennifer.

To the people who served as my "book team": Thank you for your encouragement and experience. A big thank you to the authors who shared their experiences with me and encouraged me to go for it.

To all the authors whom I have read and who have drastically affected my life's journey.

To all of the people who went ahead of me and had the courage to live their lives alive and inspired me to do the same.

CONTENTS

PREFACE

The real question is, "Do we know when we are free?"

I was sitting on a mountainside on the island of Maui when I began writing this book. As I was searching for a way to explain the idea of living alive and free, I noticed something beautiful. I looked around and realized a group of beautiful chickens were "exploring" around me. Beautiful hens, of all colors, were following one gorgeous rooster. Yes, chickens! Just roaming free! I grew up in a place where chickens don't roam free. They are kept on farms and raised for food. Did the chickens I was now seeing know they were free? I knew they were free, but did they? I think it is a gift to know you are free. Then I wondered whether the chickens that live in captivity know they are enslaved. I do know one thing—I am FREE! I am living my life alive!

I know this because there was a time when I wasn't free....

INTRODUCTION

Beginning the Journey of...
"Living Your Life Alive"

"Love the life you live. Live the life you love."

— Bob Marley

To say you are getting nowhere is an understatement. You feel like you are stuck on a treadmill. Your head is spinning and you are not getting anywhere. You are tired. You know you are worth more—called to do more—but every step leaves you in the same place. You may be tired and frustrated from supporting someone else's dream and not your own. You jog in place, worrying about what others think of you. Maybe you have never had the financial need to have to work, so you feel like you have no purpose. Perhaps it's your relationships that are strained. You have become a little bitter because you are not where you imagined you would be by now.

You have barriers in your life—you are having difficulty moving past the hurt someone caused, getting over a great loss—and you just can't feel that "breath of life" anymore. Time is just slipping away. Your life is good enough, fulfilling enough, but you know you were meant for more. You have given up on your dreams, or you are about to give up. You are falling into mediocrity! You are about to throw your arms up in the air and give up because you don't know where to turn.

Then this book somehow appeared in your life. You feel that little tingle of hope. Remember hope? Maybe it was the cover of this book or its title that caught your attention, but now you have opened it and your inner voice is speaking to you through these words. I encourage you to listen, accept this nudge, and follow it. Live your life alive! The solution is just ahead. I challenge you to choose you and follow that nudge toward your destiny.

So many things may prevent us from truly being free and living our lives alive. You may not even be able to imagine living that way. You may be asking yourself, "What does it actually feel like to live free and totally alive?"

Ask yourself: Am I financially free? Am I free to be myself in my relationships? Free to lead my family, employees, or team how I desire? Free to go about my day as I wish? Or am I tied to trading time for just enough money to get by in life? Am I free to be authentically myself? Am I free from grief? Do I live my days alive, or am I just running around inside of a wheel like a hamster in a cage? When was the last time I laughed so hard my face hurt? Ask yourself, "When was the last time I took a really deep breath just to enjoy the fresh air deep in my lungs? Is my heart free and open to love?"

I was in my late twenties when someone first asked me those questions. Thinking about them stopped me in my tracks. I was living, but I didn't feel alive, and I had stopped dreaming. Maybe you have never thought about these specific questions, but I bet you have visited these ideas or you wouldn't have picked up this book.

We are born alive, but some of us are not really living. Some of us seem to have had the "alive" part of our lives taken from us. I understand where you may be because the "alive" part of my life was gone for a while. However, I am now living more alive than ever. I followed a nudge I felt deep inside, and doing so changed my life.

Wherever you are currently, just know it is a journey. In this book, you will learn that you can overcome anything and achieve anything, but there is no secret formula or magic pill to make that happen for you. You have to be willing to do the work. Work doesn't have to be hard; in fact, it can be fun, but it is still work.

Who am I to help you? I am just a girl who chose to overcome things that, in the past, I allowed to cause me to be afraid. People often ask me how I accomplished the things I have with the obstacles that were in my way. I just found the courage to follow the nudge to move on. I believe many people have conquered much bigger obstacles to achieve higher levels of greatness than me. Even though we all have unique challenges, we all have to find the same strength and learn to follow "the nudge." This nudge is in all of us. We just have to learn to listen.

I'm also a girl who has gained insight through my personal and professional experience—experiences that help me guide you along your path. Professionally, I am an author, speaker, and coach. I have also served crime victims as a police advocate for twenty years, worked as a probation officer for five years, and mentored inside of a women's prison. Additionally, I'm an entrepreneur who has built a successful business through network marketing. I have mentored and coached hundreds of people starting their own businesses. This has led me to develop a non-profit project, Makoa Quest, a program for high-risk teens on the island of Maui.

I wrote this book to serve you on your journey. I believe it will be read by those who are supposed to read it. I'm simply the instrument bringing the message to you. This book may be easy to skim, but the real messages you need to hear will happen when you do the written exercises. If you are going to pick up this book and invest your time, I encourage you to work on and write out the exercises. During those moments, small or even large shifts will take place in your life. Reading this book may bring you inspiration, but writing will bring you transformation.

I understand you may be apprehensive about taking the first step or further steps. Maybe you have tried before and it didn't work. Maybe you haven't had the courage to live out your best life. Maybe you are overwhelmed by fear. Perhaps you don't have the support of others, or you don't believe you can do it. Is it the lack of time and focus that holds you back? Maybe it's a past failure that has a hold on you. Whatever it is, it's okay.

Throughout this book, I want to be your friend and mentor. Page by page, I want to lock arms with you. I want you to know you are not alone. It may be scary to move your life to a place where you will feel more alive, but it's okay to be scared, and the journey will be completely worthwhile.

Are you ready for me to lay the first stepping-stone at your feet? Will take the next step? Only you can decide. But if you choose to move forward—upward—I'm right here with you.

A Shields

"Every great dream begins with a dreamer. Always remember, you have within you the strength, the patience, and the passion to reach for the stars to change the world."

— Harriet Tubman

CHAPTER ONE

THE NUDGES

*"If you do not expect the unexpected, you will not find it,
for it is not to be reached by search or trail."*

— Heraclitus

So what is a nudge?

Before we jump into this explanation, if you haven't read the Introduction, please take a moment to do so. It sets up the explanation.

Nudges are when you feel that "thing" to do something that wasn't necessarily on your radar. Nudges tend to hide in moments, and then they just happen as quickly and as effortlessly as you blink. Nudges are when you feel moved by something outside of yourself to do something bigger than yourself.

The nudge is not your everyday thoughts, your truth built on years of experiences in which you have tried to avoid pain or hunger—it is not mere survival. Nudges are not the thoughts and experiences of joy or happiness. Although these thoughts and ideas are important, your conscious mind only knows some of the universal truth.

Your inner voice is the voice of your personal truth. Your mind takes in everything you see, feel, and hear, and then it sorts through it the best it can, using the information to make choices. Your inner voice is what you can hear when you quiet the noise outside and listen to your own truth and what is best for your unique self.

Our conscious mind is fallible. It makes mistakes. We may try to do the best we can along our journey, making decisions that align with living our best life. We may even have fantastic ideas at times that move us closer to our goals. But we make so many decisions each day. It seems like we make choices every few minutes. Should I hit the snooze button? Should I approach that person and make a connection? Should I allow my teenager to stay out an extra thirty minutes past curfew? Should I eat that muffin? Should I get gas now or later? Should I marry this person? All day decisions, decisions, decisions. As we grow up, we fight for the right to make decisions. I was so excited when my mom let me choose my own outfit for the first time. Now I wish my brain could turn off for a few hours and let someone else make some decisions for me. The decisions we make and the choices we are afforded are little steps in how our lives are pieced together. And sometimes these choices and decisions don't work out. One bad move and our lives can be forever changed. A single decision can change the course of history.

And then there are the NUDGES....

The nudges are different. They are unexpected and uninhibited. They are the "calling." When a nudge hits you, you are aware something is different. It is not just a good idea. It causes instant nervousness layered with peace. It's not just a tug to do this or to do that. It is piercing. It is God sent.

I call it a nudge because it feels soft, but stern. It is directional. It can be ignored, but not denied. If it's a nudge, not just an idea, you will know because you won't be able to shake it. It will keep coming up. You will see signs of it everywhere. This is the difference between a good idea and a God idea. The nudge is God's proof sent to you—showing you it is already done, all the resources are in place. The step of faith is yours to take.

We will explore the nudges throughout this book, but first, we need to look at what can hold us back from identifying and following the nudges.

CHAPTER TWO

WAKING UP TO REALITY

"If you don't like how things are, change it!
You are not a tree."

— Jim Rohn

D o you ever wonder how you got where you are right now?

Have you ever heard or seen something or been right in the middle of experiencing something when all of a sudden, you thought, "How did I end up here?"

This has happened to me a few times. I might just be going about my day when someone said something that jolted me and I thought, "How did I get here?" Think about it. How did you end up living where you live? How did you end up in the relationship (or lack of relationship) you are in (or not in) right now? How is it that you have the savings (or lack thereof) you currently have? How is it that you have spent years working at your current job? How is it that you thought high school was just a few years ago, but then you were invited to your ten-year or twenty-year reunion? How is that your kids were in diapers, but now they are growing or gone?

"I don't believe people are looking for the meaning of life as much as they are looking for the experience of being alive."

— Joseph Campbell

Sometimes, we are so wrapped up in living that we forget to live. We lose track of what is going on in our lives. Once, as a victim assistance counselor, I was on the phone with a local news personality who was also the victim of domestic violence. It was in the middle of the night, and she had called the police for help after a fight with her husband. The police had referred her to me for further assistance.

She said, "Autumn, how could this happen to me? I have covered domestic violence and I know the signs. I am a professional and should know better. How did I end up here?"

She shared a detailed account of what her partner had done over the last several years. When she finished, I helped her take immediate action to change her situation. But her words snapped me out of my optimistic slant on reality. I realized I was in the same position! I had been telling myself things would get better and he would change. But that is almost never true in cases of domestic abuse. I know this, but....

Her words were piercing, but sometimes it takes a while to make a change. I didn't take immediate action, but I couldn't shake her statement. I have learned that if you can't shake something, it usually means you need to listen because there is truth in it. Months later, after another person said something else I couldn't shake, I finally did something about my situation. Sometimes, it takes numerous people saying things in different ways to see reality. Being in a relationship that is not healthy doesn't help you stay open to feeling the nudges in your own life and creating the steps to live your life on purpose. Regardless of what type of relationship it is—family, work, or social—it can not only distract you, it can derail you!

Reality is tricky. It can hide its true self for a long time. We either encourage this by sliding on our rose-colored glasses and hoping for a brighter tomorrow, or we resign ourselves to a "Life sucks, then you die" mindset. Optimist or pessimist, there are no absolutes, but you need to be real with yourself. Time is ticking, but for us to live our lives alive, we first must know where we are in life.

Today matters! Looking at where you are today gives you a place to start and helps you see the steps you need to take to move in the direction of your dreams. Motivational speaker Les Brown says, "Too many of us are not living our dreams, because we are living our fears."

I have never met a person who was successfully living his or her life alive who didn't put some sweat into constructing the steps to get there. I would love to tell you I have the secret and all you have to do is sit on the couch, read this book, and *voilà*, you will be inspired and your life will forever be changed. That's not going to happen. It takes work and will to make the change. It takes you to decide. It takes you to take the steps needed.

John Maxwell is an author whose books I have read for years, and he has had a huge effect on my life. He has sold more than 19 million books. His book *Today Matters* took me a long time to read and was not one of my favorites. You see, John Maxwell writes mostly about leadership, and I love the study of leadership. But *Today Matters* focused on taking responsibility for your day. At the time I read it, it was hard for me to be present in a given day, much less take responsibility for it. I was either looking backwards, or more likely, I was five steps ahead of myself. Maxwell believes that today matters because it's too late for yesterday and you can't depend on tomorrow. This is why we have to focus on today.

So why do so many of us miss that? In *Today Matters*, Maxwell highlights a few reasons that I want you to consider for yourself. First, we exaggerate yesterday. Many times, our past successes and failures look bigger to us than they actually were. Some people never move past where they once were. Second, we overestimate tomorrow. Most people expect the future to be brighter than today. Most people figure tomorrow is bound to be better than today, but they don't make any changes so that can happen. Third, we underestimate today.

Maxwell says, "It all comes down to what you do today. We must focus on today." He tells us the secret to success is our daily agenda. He is not talking about a calendar or to-do list, but something much more important. "Successful people make right decisions early and manage those decision daily."

The next time reality hit me, I was on the phone with the phone/cable company. I was concerned because my account was past due. As the representative explained my options, I thought about money, bills due, and expenses that needed attention. I needed to rob Paul to pay Peter. Right then it hit me, "If I keep doing what I am doing, I am never going to have enough money for the basics, much less anything else I need or want." I was not paying the bills, let alone taking any kind of vacation—a dream vacation was out of the question. And what if the heater went out?

Well, of course, the heater did go out! It would cost $1,500 to get it fixed. I was a single parent with a space heater keeping us warm. I didn't know where to turn, or what to do. I was losing faith in myself and worrying about money, not living.

A few days later, when I went to the police department I was working for, an envelope was on my desk. Inside was a note: "We know that this doesn't cover a new heater, but we hope it helps." I cried.

I was thankful.

And I was pissed!

I never wanted to be on this side of need again. I wanted to be the one helping cover someone else's need. I looked for a way to stretch my day and work more. I looked for ways to stretch my dollars. I searched but nothing seemed to work.

A few months later, I was introduced to a different way to build a career. I started reading books, such as, *The Four Year Career: How to Make Your Dreams of Fun and Financial Freedom Come True Or Not* by Richard Bliss Brooke. This book confirmed what I already knew in many ways, but it offered even more insight. I learned to forget about the daily search for part-time jobs, to add on-top of my full-time job, and look for ways to create wealth instead. Jobs just allow you to trade time for money, but creating a business that allows you to put your time into creating wealth is a much better option.

I knew I was called to be a victim advocate, and I never worried about the money, or lack thereof, it offered. However, I did realize my finances were my responsibility, so I needed to learn more about building wealth.

Less than a year later, I resigned and showed up a week later as a volunteer doing the same job with a different police department. I knew advocating was part of who I was, but the job didn't need to define me. There was more to who I was.

I found a company I could work for part-time, working around my life and not living my life around my work. I still wanted to do what I was called to do; I just wanted to do it on my own terms and keep the other things that were important to me central. Notice, I said part-time work. Not part-time dreaming. Not part-time wishing. It was work and continues to be today. Work doesn't have to be hard, but there are usually exchanges or sacrifices that have to take place. I watch most people exchange forty years of their lives for freedom. I didn't want to wait to have the choice of how to spend my day. I wanted it sooner. I was willing to commit and work for a few years and get the same outcome. There were many days when I would wake up early before the four children. I would work for an hour or two, then go into work for eight to ten hours, offering services to crime victims in my office or on crime scenes; then I would work on my business for several hours at night and get up and do the same thing over again. There were days I was tired...really tired. There were many days when I wanted to throw in the towel. I experienced rejection over and over again in the search for like-minded people to become team members. There were many activities and events I missed out on with my family and my friends, but I knew that it wouldn't be forever. I knew what I was building was for long-term. I knew it was to build our dreams, not someone else's dream.

Evaluate where you are, be grateful, and decide whether you need to make a move. Be truthful with yourself and true to yourself!

One morning, as I was returning from walking my son to school in our suburban Denver neighborhood, I turned the doorknob and thought to myself, "I don't belong here." I had always envisioned a quaint neighborhood with lots of trees, full of diversity and community activities—a place that was friendly and kind...a place where I felt welcomed and valued. I had worked so hard for that house and to live in one of the best neighborhoods in the city. Why? It wasn't even what I wanted! The decisions I had made were lost by not managing them daily. And before I knew it, I was lost!

It is never too late to get back on track or start over!

Are you where you want to be? Have you even asked yourself

whether where you currently are is aligned with who you really are?

As I was sitting on the beach finishing writing this book, I glanced up and reality hit me again. Just out of the blue, it happened. It was like someone was saying, "Do you know where you are?" A smile emerged as I thought, "I am fully aware of where I am. I am here because I made decisions and managed them daily. I am here and I belong. I am happy. I am living my life alive!"

Exercise:

Is there an area where you are over-exaggerating yesterday or living in the past? Are you not letting go of a past failure, or are you living in the "glory days"?

_____

_____

_____

_____

_____

_____

Is there an area of your life where you are overestimating tomorrow and/or not doing anything about tomorrow today?

_____

_____

_____

_____

_____

_____

In which areas would you like to change reality?

_____

_____

_____

_____

_____

_____

_____

What decisions do you need to make so those changes can happen?

_____

_____

_____

_____

_____

_____

_____

_____

How can you manage the decision(s)?

_____

_____

_____

_____

_____

_____

_____

Do you have the skills or resources to manage the change? If so, name them:

_____

_____

_____

_____

_____

_____

_____

_____

_____

_____

_____

If not, name the skills needed and what it would take for you to increase your ability or resources:

_____

_____

_____

_____

_____

_____

_____

_____

_____

_____

_____

CHAPTER THREE

EXPERIENCING
THE UNIMAGINABLE

"Bad things can happen, and often do, but they only take up a few pages of your story; and anyone can survive a few pages."

— James A. Owen

D o you fear something? What or who is it?

Before I allowed fear to control me, I can remember a time when I enjoyed the smell of pancakes on a Sunday morning, the cold delicious taste of a snow cone in the summer, playing giddy-up horsy on my father's lap, or walking down the stairs at my grand-parents' house hearing my grandfather sing, "Here she comes... Miss America." Noticing, for the first time, the drops of dew on the bright green grass early in the morning, hearing a fast-moving river rush against the Rocky Mountain rocks. Exhilarating. Simply ex-hilarating. I didn't appreciate these simple, yet joyful experiences. Then they were gone.

I didn't even notice the joy of living had gone until I woke up to freedom after what seemed to be a lifetime later. I allowed one single incident, followed by over a decade of repeated behavior, to steal my joy and imbed fear in me....

Columbine

> *"When I despair, I remember that all through history the way of truth and love have always won. There have been tyrants and murderers, and for a time, they can seem invincible, but in the end, they always fall. Think of it—always."*

— Mahatma Gandhi

Have you ever thought about the unimaginable? Has something happened to you that you only thought happened to other people?

The alarm clock woke me to a day that would forever change the lives of thousands. I kissed my four-month-old son goodbye and hurried to work. I was working as the victim advocate for two police departments while my current post searched for my replacement and I learned the ropes at my new position. I was interviewing, along with a board, applicants to replace me. Kelly, an advocate from the county who would be assisting me with the interviewing, was sitting next to me as we waited for the chief of police and the director of human resources also to arrive for the interview. There was continuous chatter from the police dispatch center in the background.

And then it happened! Silence. All metro channels were tuned into Jefferson County, Colorado. We were just several miles away. Shots fired. Active shooting. Unknown deaths. Unknown injuries. At a high school?

Kelly and I grabbed our bags and announced we were in route. On the way, I called to check on my son. All I wanted to do was hold him and never let him go again, but right then, the community was in need. It seemed like the whole world had stopped and everything was moving in slow motion. But we needed to act fast. We were told to report to Leawood Elementary School where people were being directed to locate their high school students.

My training kicked in and I did what I was trained to do. The entire community was in shock. The media vans started pouring in from all over, and we were still trying to determine whether the shootings had stopped. Who was alive?

Cell service was immediately jammed with calls from the population of a city in crisis. I have a name for this day. I call it D-Day. It is the darkest day a parent can ever experience. Hundreds of people seeking information on their children and no information being released. A woman was clinging to me, begging me to tell her how to find her child. I didn't have any information. I watched as her husband grabbed her and tried to fix the situation for her, but there was nothing to fix.

In the end, one teacher and twelve students were killed. The frenzy of fear and loss and the joy of finding your child alive whirled around the gym. This was where parents were being directed to locate their children, not find out that their child was not there and was a victim. The gym seemed to be spinning. It wouldn't stop.

As we set up stations to gather information from the parents and organize crisis responders, Kelly and I were asked to go to the hospital to assist the wounded victims. There were twenty-one people wounded.

The dispatcher sent us to two hospitals, but we couldn't find the wounded. There were many advocates being dispatched to numerous hospitals. Where were they? How was it we couldn't find them? They were being routed to different hospitals. Give us the information! We found and were assigned to a wounded child at the third hospital. Walking into the white room, with tubes and monitors everywhere, we learned he had been shot multiple times.

But he was alive!

As we met with his parents, there were more questions than answers. Why? How? When? How many others? Has anyone been arrested? None of which we could answer. How could we answer the questions when something like this isn't even supposed to be possible? The tears of anger, sorrow, fear, and sadness continued to flow.

My pager was repeatedly going off: "911-call home." My heart sank. I called home and explained what I was doing and that I would try to get home as soon as possible.

After connecting with the wounded boy's family and assuring them we would be back with information and resources, we were called back to the elementary school. It should have been a thirty-minute drive, but it took over an hour to get through the roadblocks. As we entered the gym, it was almost silent. There were food boxes from local restaurants stacked by the hundreds against the wall. No one was eating. No one could.

Volunteers had been sorted through and assigned duties or asked to leave. Attorneys, clergy, and therapists from everywhere were asked to leave with the exception of a few. Most had good intentions, but some were vultures pulling out contracts, scheduling therapy appointments, or asking whether their church could hold the funeral services.

In the background and behind the scenes, jurisdictions and offices were fighting over who would make notifications and when. Do we tell them what is known? Does it taint the case? The suspects were dead. Many didn't know, but it had already been done.

When most of the parents had been reunited with their children and there were less than fifty parents left in the gym, still searching for their children, I was asked to go from parent to parent, asking for a physical description of his or her child. This was a different list from the one already compiled. This one was specific for the coroner's office. Of course, the parents, although suspicious, wouldn't know why I needed this info. As I circled the room, it stopped spinning. The room seemed to stand still again. I went from parent to parent. I was focused. I had a job to do. The coroner needed me to get this done and quickly. The quicker I worked, the more answers could be provided.

Getting answers didn't happen quickly. Sometimes, it didn't happen at all. I approached one family and told them I just had a few questions so we could try to provide answers for them. I asked my questions: Race. Height. Weight. Color of hair. Current picture. The mother responded, "When she walked into a room, she would light it up. She always smiled and tried to help others." Still, I didn't receive the information I needed. No description. D-Day. I had to push harder and ask more directly.

As time passed and questioning continued, I could see the parents' eyes gaze into mine, and I could see understanding as it slowly dawned. My eyes, my very own eyes, were telling the parents that asking for a physical description was not about a missing child report, but to start identifying the deceased. I looked into their eyes as parents faced the fact that their child was most likely lying dead in the school or had already been taken to the coroner's office. Could you even imagine? It was my eyes and my questions that became despised. How dare I ask questions, but have no answers. I couldn't even tell them where their child was located.

Night had fallen. People continued to whisper, and then the wailing would start again. I had never heard pain linger in the air like this.

After several hours, I finally had the information I needed. No cars were allowed in or out of the area. We had to travel by emergency or media vehicles to get in or out. A news team agreed to take me to the Justice Center.

"Excuse me," I asked one of the news personal. "Could I please use your phone to call home? My phone is dead." I needed to call home. I needed to know life was going to go on. I needed to hold my son, but I couldn't. I had to serve these families in some small, quiet way. Nothing could really help, but I was called to serve.

Hours had passed since I left the police department where I had started my day. No interviews had been conducted, no replacement found. I was still responsible for two police departments. I called to check-in with my supervisor and learned the officers had been assigned to one of the shooter's parents and their house. Legally, those parents weren't allowed advocate services. I prayed for them. I couldn't even imagine how they felt.

I was escorted to the coroner's office to hand over the descriptions. I am sure there were many people asked to get descriptions from different sources. On my way, I watched as the dispatchers were rotated to massage chairs. Many had refused to leave after their shifts and they had been working for hours. Food and massage chairs were brought to them. No one left. They just wanted to stay and help. It was the same in the field. The police and fire personnel didn't want to leave.

I was taken to the coroner's office. I handed the folders over. Thirteen folders. By the time I left, one more child had been located. That left twelve students. Later, a teacher, Dave Sanders, was identified as another victim. It was done.

The families were sent home. I was sent home. I kissed and held my son. I could breathe. However, everything about being a parent had changed that day. Everything. Really bad things can happen, even at school. I took my son to an in-home daycare and responded back to the school.

As the war between agencies over who was responsible for what raged on, I was told, along with other advocates, to respond at five in the morning so I could go to each home to do the official death notifications. The district attorney, coroner, sheriff, and police were still trying to decide who was going to do what. Maybe it wasn't a war, but it was a "first" for everyone. There was a lot of conflict, but maybe it was everyone serving with passion. Columbine was the first school crisis of this magnitude. We got through it. The notifications were made. It had all been done.

My pager was vibrating. I called the number. It was a deputy who had carried a student out of the school to safety. He wanted to know whether I thought it was a good idea for him to go visit the student in the hospital. He wanted to make sure the boy was alive, to see for himself. He didn't believe it. We had told him numerous times the student was recovering and talkative, but the officer needed to see for himself. Soon after, I watched the officer walk into his room, touch the victim on his arm, and break down. He turned with tears in his eyes, "He really is alive? So many others didn't make it." I learned later that this deputy had gone back into the school many times during the incident.

Five days had past. I had showered twice. There wasn't time to do more. No one should have to see the damage when evil rages, but thousands of us didn't have a choice. I had not been inside either police station since I was called to respond. It was time to make an appearance. I walked through the doors of Parker Police Department and said hello to my captain. He followed me into my office, shut the door behind him, and asked for the details of the past five days. I held back my tears and gave him a verbal report of the interactions. While he offered appreciation, he looked at the other cases piled up on my desk and reminded me there were others in need.

We formed a game plan, and then I left to go next door for a massage because I couldn't move my neck, and my jaw kept locking. I was hiding the pain the best I could. As I lay face down on the massage table, I sobbed. There was nothing anyone could do to fix or change anything that had happened. What surfaces are people who can care for each other through the pain.

The Power of the Human Spirit

"Owning our story and loving ourselves
through that process is the bravest thing we will ever do."

— Brene Brown

After a horrible event like the Columbine shooting, it's easy to wonder how the victims and their families, or even just the witnesses of such a horrific experience, are able to go on with their lives. But they do. As a victim advocate counselor, I have seen many horrible experiences in my life. I want to share a few of them with you so you get a full idea of the tragedy and insanity and often senseless or simply impossible to understand situations that I have witnessed in my role.

I have seen a young man accidently wrap his street bike around a tree and kill his best friend after he reluctantly gave into his friend's request to give him a ride on the back. He was later charged with a crime.

I have seen a mother have to bury her daughter after an automobile accident she caused by reaching for a pacifier in the backseat to give to her because she was crying. She crossed over the line and collided head-on with a semi-truck. She lived and her daughter didn't.

I have seen an adult son beat and scream at his dead father while being wheeled out on a gurney covered in a sheet. His father, who was an electrician, chose to hang himself with an electric cord over his and his wife's bed because he was out of work for a few weeks. I have seen a police officer have to turn away from the beating because tears were rolling down his face.

I have assisted in asking parents whether they would be willing to donate their child's organs to others in need, only minutes after they learned of their child's passing. I saw the shock on their faces as we stood in the family room of the hospital.

I have seen a young single mother make the decision to pull her daughter from life support nine days after an accident. The accident occurred after she had just picked up her daughter from her parents' house after working a night shift as a second job. On their way home, they were hit by a drunk driver. Her family told her that the reason this happened is because she chose to wear jeans the Friday before, knowing it was a sin and knowing there would be consequences. As I requested that hospital security remove her family and her church members from the room as they protested, I saw her wail over her baby girl as she took her last breaths. She knew she would be disowned and she was. Months later, as I called the young mom to talk to her about the suspect only getting a sentence of probation, I heard the wailing again.

I have had to witness an angry new mother break down after we told her that her husband was accidentally buried on a construction site. This was after the numerous calls she placed to the police begging them to do something about her husband who was a few hours late returning from work.

I have held a mother who was clinging to the hope that her child would be found after she witnessed her child being grabbed and pulled into a car as it sped off. Hours later, the child was found, but forever changed.

I have cleaned off bodily fluids from a handgun before returning it, at her request, to an elderly woman who knew it was the gun that ended her daughter's life.

I have delivered Christmas presents, on behalf of the police department, to a family of five, which was a family of six a few months prior. After laying out his highlighted life insurance policies, the father had taken his own life. During the recession, he had been denied over a hundred positions so he figured his family would be better provided for without him.

I have entered a house and seen blood dripping from the ceiling from a women who was upstairs and gave birth to her stillborn child. She was crying and silently questioning whether the child's death was due to the abuse she received at the hands of her partner, who had hit and kicked her. I have seen the eyes of the firefighter who tried to save that baby, but couldn't.

I have seen a broken women in front of me because she found out her husband was having an affair, not with another woman, but with their Chihuahua. (I can't make this stuff up.)

I have assisted a teenager in cleaning his friend's blood off his shoes after a drunken game of Russian Roulette ended in death.

I have witnessed the aftermath of a family that lost two sons at once in a boating accident during a family vacation.

I have witnessed a woman make the decision, after thirty-one years of being abused by her husband, to ask the police for help because he kicked their dog for the first time.

I have had to provide services to parents who lost their child to a sickness in the middle of the night, to later find out they were high on meth and left the sick infant by an open window with freezing temperatures blowing in. I have seen them handcuffed while they sobbed over their loss.

I watched a doctor tell a family that their loved one only has weeks to live.

I have held the hand of the woman, lying in a hospital bed, who has been raped but is fearful of reporting it.

I have stood by a family as their mother was being transported to detox for the sixth time.

I have seen a father struggling to raise his rebellious teenage daughter because his wife found someone else and left them both.

Advocates quietly serve. There were advocates who served before me who paved the road for victim's rights and created resources to support people in need. There are many more advocates serving today, and many who will serve in the future, who continue to develop programs and policies to better the process. It was an honor to serve those in need in the role of an advocate. I believe it is true human connections that help us all. We all have the power to help each other on this journey called life. Ralph Waldo Emerson said, "To know even one life has breathed easier because you have lived. This is to have succeeded."

Although I have seen the unimaginable, I have also seen the power of the human spirit.

I have seen the broken love and be loved again. I have seen the lost be found again. I have seen the hurt start movements that change not only a community, but the world. I have seen the people torn apart by tragedy be sewn back together again with the help of others who have walked down the same path. I have seen the sick and addicted heal. I have seen parks be built in remembrance and children laughing and playing ball because of that park. I have seen races put together in remembrances and fundraisers. I have seen organ donations save lives. I have seen laws change that save other lives because someone stood up and said, "We have had enough." I have seen strangers embrace in love. I have seen people who help others sleep well at night because they know they did the best they could. I have seen where one person is a light to someone else when all that person can see is darkness. I have seen where one organization accepts someone who was dismissed or disowned by another organization. I have seen people have what appears to be supernatural strength.

Throughout the years as an advocate, I have seen an enormous number of tears caused by things that just don't seem fair or things that just shouldn't happen, but they do. But I have also had the honor of seeing the power of the human spirit over and over again. The strength, the courage, the ability, and the power of the human spirit are absolutely amazing!

We all have this power in us. This power does not discriminate. You may need to dig deep to find it and identify your own strength, but it is there. I promise. It may be uncomfortable, or it might even hurt to find it, but once you find out what you are capable of overcoming or accomplishing, the gift of how strong you are is revealed and released. It can never be hidden or restrained again. Your power makes a difference. You are here for a reason.

NOT Again!

> *"The only thing necessary for the triumph of*
> *evil is for good men to do nothing."*

> — Edmund Burke

On July 21, 2012, I woke to the TV and a familiar report I remember too well. There was another mass shooting. It was at a nearby theater at the midnight screening of the film *The Dark Knight Rises.* I was glued to the television. As I watched, I reflected on what I experienced with Columbine. It was D-day all over again. It was the day when families frantically searched for answers. Were their loved ones alive? As I sat there, I told my partner, Tim, that if I hadn't retired from law enforcement, I would have been called out to serve families and I'd be gone for days. My heart ached. Shivers continued to go up and down my spine. I prayed. I prayed all day. I went about my day, knowing the families of the injured/deceased were experiencing a day that would be forever frozen in time. I knew their worlds were spinning out of control. As a prayed, I told God I would go and help if needed, and if I weren't needed, I was okay with not going, but I begged God to wrap the families in love.

It had happened again. It was done. Twelve killed and seventy injured. A person had done this again! How could this keep happening?

As I was pulling in to run a quick errand, my phone rang. It was the call. There were only certain advocates who had responded to Columbine and received the national training that came afterwards. Can one really, truly be trained or prepared for anything like a mass shooting? Was I better prepared to help this time?

For the next several hours, while attending my twentieth high school reunion, I answered phone calls from Sarah, an advocate I had trained who was on-scene and requesting some guidance. I was responsible for her training and took responsibility for helping her through D-day. I told her when you get the confirmation, you just need to meet with the family and say, "We have received confirmation that your child/brother or sister/ grandchild was killed."

She responded, "Just like that? You say it just like that?"

"Yes, exactly like that and then call me back." As an advocate, she served well. She served well for days. No amount of training can

LIVING YOUR LIFE ALIVE

help you. All you can do is take the training you received and serve "all in" with your heart.

The next morning, I responded and Sarah and I were assigned to one of the families who had lost their son. The mother and father were flying in from another state and had not received confirmation that their son was a victim. We met in a hotel conference room where I gave them confirmation that their son had been killed. I can't tell you how hard it is to get those words out of your mouth. But what I really can't imagine is being on the other side of those words. They aren't just words. They are life-altering daggers. The anger in the room was a weight like I had never felt. It had the energy of the deepest anger I had ever experienced.

I could see their inner joy instantly run out of them.

Other families gathered, many who had been there or had loved ones there who had survived. I could see the survivors' guilt in their eyes. "God, please do not let them surrender to this guilt, but know they have a purpose and let them find joy again."

My partner, Tim, and I had tickets to go see Tim McGraw and Kenny Chesney that same day. How could a concert be going on when the city was in mourning? How could I attend? I needed to breathe. From my training, I recognized that I needed to try to normalize things again. I felt like I had been sucked into a whirlwind, and I couldn't get my mind around what was happening. At the concert, a moment of silence was held in honor of all those suffering. It was unbelievable how silent an outside stadium could sound. We were standing next to a young couple when the man started crying. He showed us a picture of an x-ray, on his cell phone, of a good friend of his. At a glance, I could clearly see the bullets in the torso. When my partner opened his large arms to this stranger, the young man fell into his arms and embraced the hug. Two strangers had connected through tragedy. They took a walk to talk. Everywhere I looked, there were tears. The concert didn't help me catch my breath. It only reminded me of how far one incident can reach. It was spreading globally. The pain and fear spreads like wildfire. As crisis responders, we simply are sprinkling a few drops of water and containing nothing.

Over the next few days, we planned a viewing, a funeral, and attended the suspect's arraignment. Only thirty-five family members and advocates were allowed in the courtroom, and the rest of the seats were given to media. When the suspect was brought in, anger reared its head again. How could it not?

A few days later, a community vigil, sponsored by the City of Aurora, was held. The vigil was too much a display of politicians talking, complete with the victim's name, Alex Teves, being mispronounced. They tried. Everyone was trying, but it wasn't enough. Any attempt is not enough. The weight of the anger swept through the air again.

Even among the anger and pain, a small light shone as it was announced that three of the young men murdered had taken bullets for someone else. The community wept.

Thousands gathered and President Obama personally visited with each family. It was a nice gesture, but most people were still trying to stay awake because many had not slept for days. It was one more event they were told to attend while their lives were still spinning at warp speed.

In the days following the shooting, the media were like vultures. It was as if a huge circus had come to town, but the tents belonged to reporters. Caren and Tom Teves, who lost their son Alex, agreed to talk with national reporters under one condition. The suspect's name could not be mentioned in the same clip as the interview. Some reporters and producers agreed and some did not. However, I believe this stance was a turning point in how reporters cover mass shootings. These parents held strong and pushed for responsible reporting. They didn't just request for responsible reporting in the beginning; they pushed for it for years. Good things do come out of bad.

Two years later, at a brew fest honoring Alex Teves, there were free hug T-shirts everywhere. Alex often wore free hug T-shirts to let people know that someone cares. Hugging is not something that we just do. It is how we survive bad things in life. While I was speaking to Joann, a mother of another victim, about how anything good could come out of this tragedy or any others, she told me, "When something like this happens, you learn how deep hurt can go, but you also get to feel a love that goes even deeper."

Certain days define the rest of our lives. July 21, 2012, was one of them. Tragic events that occur in your own life or that you witness in others' lives can be life-changing, but they don't have to define who you are. You are worth all the moments in your lifetime. Some of the best moments of your life are still to come, but you must believe it.

Unforeseen incidences that injure you deeply cause you to question life; they inject fear into you, infuse your mind with confusion, and can seem to overturn the plans you had for your life, but many times, these very instances are where your own strength and greatness is discovered. Honor the process of healing and make the decision to be the best *you* through that process. How you view and experience the unforeseen things that happen can open you up to experiencing the power of the human spirit, or it can seem to break you. It seems when fear, of any kind, takes hold in your life, that it can stop you in your tracks from being able to move forward. Could you take a look at your own fear and be open to experiencing your very own power?

Exercise:

Do you believe bad things can happen to "undeserving" people? Has someone caused you pain you didn't deserved?

_____

_____

_____

_____

_____

List the people and/or incidences:

_____

_____

_____

_____

_____

Are you willing to forgive?

_____

_____

_____

_____

_____

_____

We know bad things happen but good can come out of them. What has happened to you or what have you witnessed where good came from bad?

_____

_____

_____

_____

_____

_____

_____

_____

_____

_____

_____

_____

CHAPTER FOUR

FEAR: THE GIFT THAT KEEPS ON GIVING

"You know my name, not my story.
You've heard what I've done, but not what I've been through."

— Jonathan Anthony Burkett

G oogle defines fear as an unpleasant emotion caused by the belief that someone or something is dangerous, likely to cause pain, or a threat. Anxiety is a prolonged feeling of helplessness, hopelessness, and/or sadness. It is important for us to differentiate between fear and anxiety.

How we react to fear can keep us safe, keep us alive, or hurt us. We usually react to fear in two basic ways: fight or flight.

The fight-or-flight response (also called the fight, flight, freeze, or fawn response or hyper-arousal) is a physiological reaction that happens when we perceive danger or a threat to our survival. The term was coined by Walter Bradford Cannon, who described it in relation to how animals' nervous systems prime the animal to fight or flee by releasing hormones that trigger those responses.

The California Science Center suggests we have to react quickly to potential danger in order to stay safe. Once the brain jumpstarts the fear response, physiological changes begin to affect the entire body.

First, the sensory organs, which include our eyes, ears, tongue, nose, and skin, pick up cues from our surroundings and feed them to the brain.

The brain's threat center, a structure called the amygdala, is constantly on the lookout for danger. It identifies a possible threat. It sounds the alarm and kicks the fight or flight response into gear. Before we know it, we are taking quick, shallow breaths, our heart starts to beat faster, and we begin to sweat. We are looking for a quick getaway or a way to defend ourselves.

All of us have developed different fears at different levels. Many fears are minor, so we can identify them and have a good grip on moving past them. Examples in our own lives could be walking into a networking group for the first time or jumping into the deep end of the pool.

> Then we have the F.E.A.R. that is False Evidence Appearing Real. These are the things that tend to paralyze us, but they will usually not actually happen. Think about all of those things you have worried about that could have happened, but never did. Think about all of the things that

consume your thoughts now that most likely will never happen, but you allow thoughts of these things, not reality, to take up space in your head and alter your decisions in life, for example, worrying about the bridge that could collapse as you drive to work or a disease that could take a family member away, even though that person is perfectly healthy.

Then we have the fears that are very real and can take the breath right out of us. It's hard to live your life alive when you don't have air! This is when bad things happen to us; they may be unlikely to happen again, but fear embeds itself into our beings. The quicker we deal with these fears, the better. For example, if you were in a car accident, every time you walk up to your car to get in, you relive the impact and it takes the air right out of you. Maybe it's hearing a loud noise and reliving the IED exploding when you were serving in Iraq. Perhaps it's seeing the person who did the unimaginable act to you and you know it's possible that he or she will do it again.

Regarding fear that is caused by something in the past, you can always do something to help you put it in the past and stop reliving the experience over and over. Many professionals and tools can help with this. You don't have to live a life of reliving things. Where the threat is still present, you can almost always do something about it, too. That is what I did. I got sick and tired of being anxious and not feeling joy. For too long, I felt like I had no air left in me. I knew if I wanted something to change, I would need to do something differently.

Fear comes in all shapes and sizes; however, we are only born with two fears. The two innate fears are fear of falling and fear of loud noises. You may have developed other fears over your lifetime, such as fear of success or failing. Perhaps it's the fear of being inadequate? Or fear of being abandoned or never loved like you deserve. Do you fear losing all of your possessions? Do you fear you won't make the cut or the team?

Change the story...change your life. Fear will keep you unhappy the rest of your life if you let it.

You can either kick fear out of your heart and mind or let it keep you from prospering! You can choose to live a mundane life or a miraculous life.

There is nothing more powerful than your choice. You are so powerful. You can travel on the road of fear or travel on the road of faith, but you can't be on both at the same time.

Exercise:

Can you identify an area where you are experiencing anxiety or fear?

_____

_____

_____

_____

_____

_____

_____

_____

Are you willing to move past the fear? Yes or no?

_____
_____
_____
_____
_____
_____
_____
_____

Are you willing to commit to what it takes to do so?

_____
_____
_____
_____
_____
_____
_____
_____

CHAPTER FIVE

FAILING FORWARD

"There is freedom waiting for you, on the breezes of the sky, and you ask, 'What if I fall?' Oh but my darling, What if you fly?"

— Erin Hanson

There are all types of anxiety or fear you can experience. What is it that is holding you back?

If your dreams don't scare you, they are probably not big enough. In most cases, people don't live their lives alive because they fear success or failure.

People who fear success may fear the responsibilities that come along with it. Does this sound like you? Do you fear that more eyes will be on you with even more expectations? Do you feel like you will have a bigger target on your back and be opening yourself up to more criticism? Do you know that the more you succeed, the more your circle of influence will grow, and you just don't know whether you are ready for that?

People who fear failure are paralyzed by the thought of taking any step toward their goals. Do you only attempt things you know you can achieve? Does just the thought of failing make you feel a pit in your stomach? Do you do things that you know you are capable of without having to depend on others?

Today, James Clear is a successful writer and has published several e-books, including *The 7 Pillars of Successful Living*, but when he began writing, he may have feared both success and failure. Here he describes the fear he initially felt:

Long before I was publishing articles for the world to read, I wrote in a private document. I did this for more than a year. There were a variety of reasons and excuses that I used to rationalize why I wasn't sharing my writing with others, but in many ways it boiled down to fear.

Here's what I didn't realize at the time: fear isn't something that must be avoided. It is not an indicator that you're doing things wrong. Fear is simply a cost that all artists have to pay on the way to doing meaningful work.

I encourage you to get on the treadmill, or whatever it is in your life, next to someone who is going just a little faster than you and who is in a little better shape than you.

I know you have been told before to rub elbows with those more successful than you, but are you doing it in all areas of your life? Sometimes we find value in helping others, but we also need help if we are going to grow. The only way to fail is failing to ask. I know, I know...you may not like others helping you or having to admit you need help. Well, you cannot go where you want to go by being the same person you are today. We all need each other in order to grow and learn from each other. The best of the best have mentors, teachers, consultants, trainers, and/or guides. Nineteenth century British poet Christina Rossetti once asked, "Can anything be sadder than work left unfinished? Yes, work never begun."

If you let fear win, you will fail. If you have ever said, "I know what giving up feels like," then today, say instead: "I want to see what happens if I don't give up." Everything is possible! You are far too smart to be standing in your own way! What if you could stop visualizing the penalties of failure and visualize the rewards of living your life alive? Just imagine a life of freedom instead of captivity!

World famous minister Joel Osteen sells out places like Yankee Stadium and speaks live to 40,000 people a week. Osteen said the week before his first sermon in 1999 marked the worst days of his life. "I was scared to death," he said. At the time, he knew very little about speaking or preparing a message. In fact, he was perfectly content to sit behind the video camera during his father's sermons. When his father passed away, Osteen's wife and family encouraged him to take the stage. Osteen did not overcome his fear for a long time. The conversations he heard didn't help. "I overheard two ladies say, 'He's not as good as his father.' I was already insecure and—boom—another negative label." Words, Osteen says, are like seeds. If you dwell on them long enough, they take root and you will become what those words say you'll become—if you let them. Osteen says negative labels—the ones people place on us and the labels we place on ourselves—prevent us from reaching our potential.

I find that leaders who are nervous about speaking in public say the most awful things to themselves—words that they would never say to anyone else. I've heard leaders say:

- "I'm terrible at giving presentations."
- "I got nervous once and it ruined me. I'm a horrible public speaker."
- "Nobody wants to listen to me. I'm boring."

If these are the types of phrases you repeat to yourself day after day, it's no wonder you get nervous! You can't control what other people say about you, like the two women Osteen overheard, but you can control how you frame those comments, and you can most certainly control the things you tell yourself. Osteen said those negative labels played in his mind again and again: "*You're not good enough. You don't have what it takes. Those women are right; you'll never be as good as your father.*" Osteen's confidence grew as he replaced those negative labels with words of encouragement, empowerment, and strength. "Wrong labels can keep you from your destiny," he says.

Choose your words wisely. Speak life into your life even when you don't know for sure or 100 percent believe that it will happen. If it's possible, say it! Your words can double as self-fulfilling prophecies. Mark Batterson shares that negative prophecies are validated by fear. Positive prophecies are validated by faith. Do you ever hear people say they are never going to find a good job, lose that weight, or find that special someone, and they never do? He illustrates this by sharing the story of Hall of Fame baseball pitcher, Gaylord Perry, who made a comment before stepping into the batter's box. He said, "They'll put a man on the moon before I hit a home run." Gaylord Perry hit the first and only home run of his baseball career six years later on July 20, 1969—just a few hours after Neil Armstrong set foot on the moon! What home run could you be hitting if you believed in yourself?

"A bird sitting on a tree is never afraid of the branch breaking because her trust is not on the branch, but on her wings."

— Author Unknown

Exercise:

Do you have a fear of failure or a fear of success?

_____

What is the worst thing that could happen to you by taking the next step?

_____
_____
_____
_____
_____
_____
_____

What is the best thing that could happen to you by taking the next step?

_____
_____
_____
_____
_____
_____
_____

What is it costing you in life not to take the next step?

_____
_____
_____
_____
_____
_____
_____

Who could you learn something from about where you want to go? (Perhaps a mentor in the field you want to grow in. Someone who has been where you are and is on the other side of it. Perhaps a person who gives you insight into having a better marriage, better finances, or being a better parent.) Important: Don't take advice from someone more messed up than you are.

_____
_____
_____
_____
_____
_____
_____
_____
_____
_____
_____
_____
_____
_____
_____
_____
_____

CHAPTER SIX

PLAYING IT SAFE

"Playing safe is probably the most unsafe thing in the world.
You cannot stand still. You must move forward."

— Robert Collier

We all play it safe at different times in different situations. Maybe because we act like we believe others want us to act or we are just trying to fit it. We wrap ourselves in a package that will be socially acceptable. Maybe we believe playing it safe won't stir the pot or ruffle anyone's feathers. Maybe it's because we have grown complacent. I observe and sometimes fall into the same trap of only asking for things to which I know I am going to get the answer "Yes." I watch as people want something, but won't ask for what they need because they are afraid of the answer "No." They play it safe. All of the people I know who are living their dreams, from the success they created, heard "No" many more times than the person who is playing it safe. However, the end result is that it is not the person with only the "yeses" who wins, but it's the person who has heard many "Nos." What is your excuse? International speaker Rita Davenport said, "Get your ask in gear." What does it hurt to ask? What does it hurt to try?

I believe most of the time we play it safe it's because we fear playing big instead of small. What if we played all out and all in? What would it feel like for us to play big at work, in our businesses, in our family, in our social groups? What would it feel like to be loved and accepted, playing ourselves and playing big?

I encounter people every day, as I am sure you do, who are not living up to their potential. I bet if I asked you whom you know who is not living up to his or her potential, you could name a few. In fact, watching these people not live up to their potential probably causes you some amount of frustration. People in your life are applying for jobs that are easy to get, but are not good fits for them. People are running businesses that could be so much more, but they play it safe by just doing enough. People date or get married to others who hold them back instead of helping them fly. People live somewhere they don't like, but they are afraid to move somewhere new. So frustrating!

But what about you? Change starts with acknowledging that the life you're living doesn't line up with the life you want. From there, it's about getting off autopilot!

Playing the victim role does not serve you. Please don't take this the wrong way. I am not saying that something horrible didn't happen to you. I served as a victim advocate for almost two decades. I have seen some of the most horrific things happen to people. People hurt people, but how does taking on the role or identity of a victim serve you? If it does, how? Let me ask you whether taking on a survivor identity serves you better? By choosing to overcome what happened and living your best life, you will not only change the course of your life, but you will change the course of so many others. You will be an inspiration by letting others know you are worth an amazing life, which is so much more important.

You can't play big in life and play the victim role at the same time. However, you can say, "This happened; watch me overcome it." I am not saying what happened will go away. It is a process, and that process needs to be honored. The good news is that it's your story—you can write the next chapter. However, you can't start writing the next chapter if you are too busy re-reading the last one. Give yourself permission and time to start writing the next chapter.

Maybe one of these stories is part of your story. What your boss did was not fair. Cancer tried to rob you of life. Someone close to you was taken way too soon. You trusted that partner and he or she betrayed you. You gave your money to someone you trusted and you lost it. You fought in a war and you are still trying to put the pieces back together. You were abandoned. Your parents divorced and it turned your world upside down. You were just minding your own business when tragedy struck. Don't take the bait! These things try to catch you and completely sidetrack you from your purpose. Let go of the bait! Recognize it and know that who you are is bigger than anything that has happened to you. It is true. It may not seem like you are bigger than what is going on, but you have a very powerful spirit and your purpose matters!

What do you need to let go of to play bigger?

On Borneo, the natives have a unique way of catching monkeys. They use a hollowed out coconut and some green bananas—the monkeys' favorite treat. In one end of the coconut, they make a hole just big enough for an adult monkey's open hand. They tether the other end of the coconut to a tree. Then they drop a banana into the coconut and scatter some around to bait the monkeys.

When a troop of monkeys shows up, one monkey will invariably find the coconut and stick in a hand and grab the banana. The monkey is then trapped. Not in the sense that the monkey can't get away—all it has to do is let go of the banana, after all. But when the villagers show up the next day, they almost always find the monkey battered and bruised or dead of exhaustion because it spent its energy struggling to free its hand without releasing its grip.

Now, you may think this tactic wouldn't work on people, but many, if not most of us, find ourselves trapped by material possessions, positions of power, or other "needs" from which we cannot free ourselves. Our trap may be a job we believe we need, a house we feel we must have, drugs we are addicted to, an incident that happened to us and we won't let go of that identity, or a partner whom we can't seem to let go.

Think about your life.

What are you trapped by?

Are you a monkey? No. If you were trapped and you heard the villagers coming for you, could you cut off your hand and run for it? You don't have to: You can open your hand and let go.

We also tend to play within our understanding of what is possible.

When presented with a puzzle, do you look at it from your current understanding of what is possible, or do you look at it and think, "What else is possible?"

In his book, *The Grave Robber*, Mark Batterson explains the difference between convergent and divergent thinking. Convergent thinking is whittling away at a problem until you find the solution to it. Divergent thinking doesn't look for one correct answer; instead, it comes up with as many solutions as possible. Are you open to as many solutions as possible?

Playing small can feel safe, but it is painful. You feel the pain of regret instead of feeling the rush of doing the very thing that you know can change your life. Imagine feeling satisfied from feeding that burning desire to be more.

Baseball player, Babe Ruth, was not only the home run king; he was the strikeout king, too.

Michael Jordan said, "I've missed more than 9,000 shots in my career. I've lost almost 300 games. Twenty-six times I've been trusted to take the game winning shot and missed. I've failed over and over and over again in my life. And that is why I succeed."

Walt Disney had his first beloved character—Oswald the Lucky Rabbit—stolen from him and Disney had to declare bankruptcy. Nevertheless, he was bold and brave enough to try again. Walt drew a mouse, named it Mickey, started Disney Studios, and never looked back.

In 1992, Jeff Bezos had a cushy job making big bucks on Wall Street when he discovered that the Internet was growing at 2,300 percent a year. He must have known boldness is a requirement of the game: He quit his job, his wife McKenzie drove them West to Seattle while he pounded out a business plan on a laptop, and they started the first ever store on the Internet—a little something called Amazon.com.

Now I know what you are thinking. You are saying, "But I'm not Michael Jordan." You are right. You are not! You are uniquely made with your own unique talents and abilities. This is your life. This is your time. Your life matters just as much as the next person's. What are you going to do with it?

Get over yourself. Everyone else has.

My life changed when I decided to put away my fears and follow the nudges. I decided to take the steps necessary to succeed. I decided to take a risk. I decided to allow people to think I was crazy (they weren't paying my bills anyway). I decided, tremblingly I might add, to go where I was nudged.

"Someone once told me not to bite off more than I can chew. I told them I would rather choke on greatness than nibble on mediocrity."

— Author Unknown

I am writing my thoughts on this page and sending it out to the world. It will mark a moment in time or maybe even a place in history. Maybe my name will not be known by the world like Michael Jordan's name is, but maybe it will. Why not yours?

Heck, Colonel Harland David Sanders went from selling fried chicken on the side of the road to creating one of the largest food empires in the world, and only after the age of sixty-five did he take his restaurant and franchise it nationally and internationally. That is the abbreviated version of his story, which is well-known. What many don't know is what happened between the chickens on the roadside and his thousands of restaurants. Colonel Sanders lived boldly as a small child. He had many careers and he learned what he wanted and what he didn't want. He suffered personal and professional heartache. One of his children died and his first restaurant and motel was lost to a fire.

We tend only to see the result, the success story, or the perfect life portrayed on Facebook. What if we could see the minutes of someone's life instead of just his or her title or result? We tend to compare ourselves to everyone else's success, but we judge ourselves by our minutes.

I'm not the same gender, color, size, age, nor do I have the same abilities as Michael Jordan, but I am amazing. You are amazing. Each one of us is so important. Your life matters!

Well, I can't throw a ball or make a basket, and you definitely don't want to taste my cooking, but I can show you what can happen if you follow the nudge.

Exercise:

Can you identify an area where you are playing it safe?

_____
_____
_____
_____
_____
_____
_____

What is the worst thing that could happen if you chose to play it big?

_____
_____
_____
_____
_____
_____
_____
_____

What is the best thing that could happen to you by playing it big?

_____
_____
_____
_____
_____
_____
_____

What is it costing you to play it safe?

_____

_____

_____

_____

_____

_____

_____

_____

CHAPTER SEVEN

WAITING ON OTHERS OR NOT

"In my moments of doubt, I've told myself firmly:
If not me, who? If not now, when?

— Emma Watson

A re you ready?

In this chapter, I am giving you permission to do two things:

1. Take action before you are prepared.
2. Not wait on other people or get permission.

It's a terrible thing to wait until you are ready. There's almost no such thing as ready. There's only now, and generally speaking, you may as well do it now. It is okay to take action before you are fully prepared, fully equipped, graduated, certified, or promoted. I hear people say, "I don't know enough." We all feel that way at times. We learn by going through it, whatever "it" is. It is like sitting through a year of geometry and never doing a proof. We have to do the proof, whether correct or incorrect, to learn. Life is an internship!

I'm not asking you to plunge in, but I am asking you to get your feet wet. We learn a lot just by stepping in the water. When are we ever really ready? When do we really have everything we need? When I felt the nudge to move and start my own business, I had to trust that all the resources I needed were already waiting. Are you waiting for the resources to show up before you move? I encourage you to walk in faith. If it is a nudge, the resources will be there.

They say you should always listen to your parents, but I'll bet Joe Green wishes he hadn't. Joe decided to stay in college instead of dropping out with his roommate Mark Zuckerberg to create Facebook.

It was a billion dollar mistake. After creating a Hot-or-Not style website at Harvard called Facemash, the two got into trouble with the university, and Joe's dad warned him not to get involved in another project with Mark.

If Joe had got on board in those early days, he would have had about a 5 percent stake, which would be worth about $7 billion today.

Although it is a sad story for Joe, could you imagine if Mark had waited for Joe? Or what if he waited for someone else to tell him what to do next? Not only would his life be different, but the world would be without Facebook. Could you even imagine? Mark wasn't ready. He was a student, but he had a vision.

One day, Walt Disney took his friend Art Linkletter out to the country. They drove deep into the countryside and stopped the car. Walt told Art about the things he was going to build and asked Art to buy the adjoining land. Art didn't see how Walt would get people to drive twenty-five miles into the woods, so he passed. Walt told Art he could handle the development himself, but the land all around his project would be filled with hotels and restaurants in just a few years. Art could get the land cheap and it would be worth a fortune when Walt's project took off.

Art tells it this way: "What could I say? I knew he was wrong! I knew that he had let this dream get the best of his common sense, so I mumbled something about a tight-money situation and promised that I would look into the whole thing a little later."

Art didn't buy the land. Walt followed his dream—he built Disneyland and raised the bar for what people expect from amusement parks and entertainment.

You can't wait for people to get on your bandwagon. You need to drive that bandwagon around and let everyone hear what you have to play!

Not everyone is going to hop on, and that's okay. They may find their own bandwagons. Others may not find anything and be left behind. Once you are driving your bandwagon, what you leave behind can be hard, especially if someone close to you decides not to come along. You may be willing to live your calling while he or she may not. You may be willing to live outside of your comfort zone when others may not. You may have resources that they do not. You may have support that they do not. You may be willing to risk and they may not. It is okay. We are all on our own journey, but you can't wait. You have permission to move forward. Be the inspiration.

Prepare for Impact

After a few years in my networking business, I was at an all-time high. Things were only going up. The economy was thriving and business was rocking. Then it happened. Well, many things happened and my life was rocked! The economy crashed. House prices dropped. People were getting laid off by the thousands across America. My business took a dip. My husband, Philip, returned from Iraq and my world slowly unraveled. We lost our authentic selves and, therefore, each other. My world was rocked and I mean rocked! I had divorced my son's dad nine years earlier, and never imagined that I would go through another divorce. I had worked hard to build a future with my son, my husband, and his three children. The dreams I had for our future crumbled. It took a while, but I had to start dreaming different dreams. I had to dig deep and find reasons to keep going, to keep loving, to keep working at building my business and to keep dreaming.

Remember the famous crash into the Hudson River. The U.S. Airways jet landed in the Hudson River near Manhattan on a Thursday afternoon, plunging its 158 passengers and crew into freezing waters. Miraculously, everyone on board escaped, thanks to pilot Chesley "Sully" Sullenberger of Danville, California, who managed an incredible water landing. "Prepare for impact" was all the pilot said before the craft landed in the river, according to passenger Alberto Panero in a phone interview with CNN's Wolf Blitzer. Are you prepared for the next impact that hits your life? I wasn't. I was young, successful, and living the dream. Impact happened. I wasn't prepared. Many of us have experienced dips in business, divorce, illness, layoffs, health issues, or loss. We can never prepare for all of the bad things that could happen, but we can prepare by doing what we have control over. This helps us feel less stress, stay present, and not worry about the past or future. Do not wait on others to prepare. Take control. It's your life!

I've had numerous people tell me they will join me in business— someday. Or move to Maui with me—someday. Or help me with the non-profit project I started—someday. What if I had waited? My bank account, where I live, and where I serve would all be on hold. The times I have waited for other people proved to be a bad idea. We can't hit the hold button while we wait for someone else's "someday" to arrive.

Are you prepared for the great things in life that happen? Such as that new relationship, career opportunity, baby, or the opportunity to serve by giving. Are you prepared for the nudge? Remember that thing you feel and know you are just supposed to do it? Are you in a place where you can accept that nudge? Prepare for impact. Don't wait on others. Ask people to come along or move along!

Have you ever skipped a rock across a body of water? I'm sure if rock-skipping were an actual sport, my father could have gone to the Olympics and won! He is a pro rock skipper. I was always mes- merized by how one point of impact could cause awesome ripples to develop and waves to shake across the water. What is your point of impact? Doing what you are called to do is your point of impact. The ripples are your effect on others. Regardless of what you did or are going to do, your courage is the point of impact and has a ripple effect. Your courage shakes people around you and activates their courage. It's not just the specific thing you do that makes the difference, although it may have an effect on many; it is you who causes it. By following your nudge, that project, business, or relationship change, you affect others, and there will be ripples that you will hear about. There will also be ripples you never hear about, but they were because of you.

If you want to be taken seriously by others, you not only need to have passion and be a vision-caster, but you need to be consistent with your work. People are watching. Give them a good show. You want people to support your dreams, so you need to prove yourself by being consistent with your own work. Those people at the top of the mountain didn't fall there, and you won't either. Climb your mountain, not to show others you can do it, but as an inspiration to others and so you can have a better view of the world.

People will move out of your way if you know where you are going. Walk away from people who are not serving your greater self and what you are called to do.

Exercise:

Is there something that you would like to do or you feel called to do that you are not prepared for right now?

_____

_____

Is moving forward now an option?

_____
_____
_____
_____

Is there someone else you are waiting on to move forward with your dream(s)? If so, who?

_____
_____
_____
_____
_____

Are you seeking permission from someone to move forward with your dream(s)? If so, who?

_____
_____
_____
_____
_____
_____

What ripple effect could happen if you move forward?

_____
_____
_____
_____
_____
_____

CHAPTER EIGHT

MASKING OUR FACES

"We all wear masks and the time comes when we cannot remove them without removing some of our own skin."

— Andre Berthiaume

Wat are you masking in your life? What mask are you hiding behind?

Dig deep. We all have masks we wear. Most people want to make good impressions and show their best selves. Some of us have multiple masks. I wore one of my masks for years. I wore the mask of joy to cover the face of fear.

Can you identify with any of the following masks:

1. I have it all together...when you don't.

2. Not having enough money is fine with me...when you know more money would be beneficial.

3. I have money, the house, the car...when your debt is suffo-cating you.

4. I live a healthy lifestyle...when you are eating crap when no one is watching.

5. My family life is great, as you can see from my Facebook page...when things are falling apart at home.

6. I live healthy and whole...but you're hiding an addiction.

7. I tell others I serve my family...but behind the scenes, you don't provide financial or emotional support.

8. I love myself...when you feel guilty for doing something nice for yourself.

9. I'm successful and confident...but you're not comfortable in your own skin.

Behind every perfect mask is a perfect mess. It's okay not to be okay. It's also okay to be you, just the way your are. You are uniquely made.

When I wore the mask of joy, but only felt fear, breathing didn't come easy. I tried my best just to breathe. I would attempt to take another breath, but I couldn't take too deep of a breath because I might feel it again—the discomfort of breathing behind a mask and feeling the fear straining itself from wanting to show through. It was exasperating. I can't allow myself to feel. I am just allowed to live. Fear sometimes allows life, but never allows living. By taking short shallow breaths, I can just keep moving. If I take too deep of a breath, someone might be able to hear that my breath breaks or my chest quivers. If I breathe too deep, someone might recognize my pain and the lack of will I have to live. I have mastered this type of breathing. I don't really know whether anyone notices. For the past decade, I was "on the go" all of the time. I had to keep the mask on! I knew that if I removed the mask, people would see that I was hurt, devastated, broken, and lived in constant fear. Masks can block our ability to connect and experience peace and love.

I lived in fear because of one incident, and then, for the next decade and a half, and through continuous other incidences, I believed it to be proof of why I should live in fear. When false allegations were cast upon me, fear became imbedded. People who try to hurt others or even attempt to destroy someone else, do it in all different ways. Fear of any kind can hinder the way you make decisions and affect the way you live.

How does this happen?

Many times, we just start spinning the wheel of psychological masks and we lose our identity. Our minds start saying we should look like this, act like this, love like this. Like or dislike that, believe in that, live like that, and if we can't meet those expectations, then many times we think a mask is the answer. It's all we know. I encourage you to be open to other options and other solutions. First, you need to get comfortable just being you. Maybe you need to stop right now and start getting to know yourself...your real self.

Many times, masks develop out of hurt, rejection, tragedy, or loss, and you may think you need to interact with the world in a certain way so your wear a mask. For me, it took a very long time to find the courage to remove my mask and let people see that there was no joy on the inside. It took years for me to trust anyone, to breathe any kind of deep breath, and to show the fear. I was embarrassed because it was my choices that put me in the situation in the first place. It took me years to step out and let everyone see the behind-the-scenes version of me. One time, one of my friends made a comment that I was a "hot mess." The nerve of that girl! I actually asked her to meet me for lunch to let her know that she hurt my feelings and I thought her comment was inappropriate. As we met, she explained that she thought the world of me and that being a mess doesn't make you any less of a person. How could I not be a mess? I was right in the middle of a divorce and my heart was broken. We can all allow ourselves to be a mess. More people will benefit from seeing you a mess and how you overcome it, than if you have it all together all of the time...or at least pretend that you do.

It took even longer for me to step up and let everyone see my strengths and my light. It doesn't benefit you in any way to hide behind any mask or beat yourself for why you are there in the first place. The only thing that benefits you is serving your authentic self and sharing you with the world.

One thing that can hold you back from letting everyone see your light is judgment of yourself and others. Judgment is the forming of an opinion, estimate, notion, or conclusion based on a set of circumstances.

We've all heard that we shouldn't judge others, but while the Bible warns us, "Judge not, lest ye be judged," the real disadvantage to judging others is that we're spending time worrying about other people's problems when we could be spending that time improving ourselves. Focusing our energy on judging others prevents us from having a healthy spirit of self-examination and, consequently, of self-improvement. The person who continually pries into other people's affairs must neglect his own. So the person who looks out constantly with a critical eye on others' motives is often unaware of his own. Of course, we can benefit by contemplating—not judging—others. That benefit can be summed up in an old Roman proverb: "Look into men's lives as into looking-glasses." That is, don't judge others but seek to see yourself reflected in them. See them in their trials and temptations, see them in crises of thought and action, and consider how you would have fared in similar circumstances. This will help you to solve the great problem and goal of life, which ultimately is to "Know thyself."

As we examine how we judge others, we need to look at how we judge ourselves. How do you judge yourself? Do you give yourself grace, or are you extremely critical of yourself? What if you could look at your self-judgments with interest and curiosity? Notice how you feel when you are thinking a thought of judgment. Does it cause you to be anxious or upset? Do you feel excited to learn more and explore more? Perhaps you just get giddy with delight when thinking about yourself.

When judging yourself, much of that judgment comes from what you think others may think of you. I've come to the conclusion that if I did everything "right" to impress people, maybe half the people would like me and half wouldn't. But if I did nothing to impress them and was just myself, maybe half the people would like me and half wouldn't. So why bother working so hard to gain their approval? Work on gaining your approval.

Each time you notice yourself judging others or judging yourself, try to "change channels" by shifting your thinking into something truer and more positive. Try to give people and intentions the benefit of the doubt when their actions upset you. Try to give yourself grace and watch what happens. After I implemented this tool of intentionally changing the channel, in about a year, something very magical happened: I stopped judging myself and others. Of course, judgment still seeps in sometimes, but I am aware of it instantly and change the channel. Not only did I stop judging myself, but I also stopped needing others' approval. Because I was now valuing myself instead of judging myself, the actual need for others' approval went away. The thought of others even thinking of me soon melted away. What a relief! I soon realized that by judging myself and trying to do what I thought others would want, I wasn't succeeding in controlling how others felt about me. Can you believe it? The fact is that regardless of how I acted, I couldn't control others, and neither can you. When we judge ourselves or others harshly, it tends to lean our thoughts and actions toward negativity. How can we truly live our life alive when we are beating ourselves or everybody else up? Although judging seems to come naturally, you can learn to replace it with grace.

This process helped me accept other people as they are and not wish to change anyone; instead, I began to celebrate others for their good points. If you are judgmental toward others, it may be you are not accepting and celebrating yourself. When you become less judgmental of yourself, tolerance is born in so many different areas. Out of tolerance comes discovery and celebration of self and others. It is amazing what you miss out on when you stand in judgment instead of acceptance. Allow yourself to move into a place of acceptance in any area of your life where you are standing in judgment.

The best gift you can give someone else is to show him or her your authentic self. Why in the world would you want to be anyone else anyway? Everyone but you is already taken. To live your life alive, you must live the life you were meant to live, not someone else's.

Will you take off your masks and lay them down? The world is waiting. Just be you and be the best you.

Exercise:

What are you masking?

_____
_____
_____
_____
_____

Why?

_____
_____
_____
_____
_____
_____

LIVING YOUR LIFE ALIVE

What mask(s) would you remove if you knew it was safe?

_____
_____
_____
_____
_____
_____
_____

If you laid down your masks, what would your life look like?

_____
_____
_____
_____
_____
_____
_____
_____
_____

CHAPTER NINE

STEPPING INTO THE RING

"Courage is not the absence of fear, it's overcoming it."

— Natalie Dormer

What are you avoiding that you know you need to do?

When has an obstacle caused you to step aside or run away?

Sometimes, the very thing we don't want to do is the very thing we must do. Ask yourself: What am I doing today that is getting me closer to where I want to be tomorrow?

The movie We Bought a Zoo, starring Matt Damon, tells the true story of a single dad who decides his family needs a fresh start, so he and his two children move to the most unlikely of places: a zoo. The zoo is badly in need of improvement and the animals need better care, but by pulling together, the family and a few staff members turn the dilapidated zoo into a family attraction and a profitable enterprise again. The courage the family shows is also relevant to a scene when the son is seeking his father's advice on how to ask out a girl. He tells his son, "You know, sometimes all you need is twenty seconds of insane courage. Just literally twenty seconds of just embarrassing bravery. And I promise you, something great will come of it." Courage is contagious!

We put many things off because of fear. We may fear being hurt, fear the unknown, fear losing our battle with illness, fear losing our loved ones, or fear losing the respect of people whom we respect. The list goes on with many real and not so real reasons for why we just don't step into the ring and do what we need to do.

One tool that I have recently found is the five-second rule. I viewed a TED talk by Mel Robbins. Her talk, "How to Stop Screwing Yourself Over," simply sums up what so many of us suffer from, but she gives us a "no excuses" way to solve it. She first asks you to choose what you want. Just choose. Then know that getting what you want is simple, not easy, but simple. We live in an amazing time. There is information on anything we want to do and endless resources.

The fact that God put you here is amazing, so, of course, it stands to reason that God would also give you life-changing ideas. If you are in your own head, you are behind enemy lines. That is not God talking. Your feelings about things are screwing you. Mel believes what happens is that our brain functions on autopilot; for example, when you pull into work and think, "Wow, I don't even remember driving here," that is autopilot. When a new idea is introduced, regardless of what it is, an emergency brake goes off. Her secret to overcoming the brake so you can live your life alive is that you have five seconds to do something about it. Within five seconds, your emergency brake will give you a list of reasons why you shouldn't. No one told us when we were eighteen that we were going to have to parent ourselves. We have to force ourselves to do things we don't feel like doing.

When you are scared to pick up that phone and call a potential client, to meet with someone and say what you need to say, to file the paperwork, to call that person and ask him or her out, to launch that website and show the world you are in business, to say, "I love you," just find those few seconds of insane courage and do it.

Just imagine if you could take advantage of those few seconds of insane courage and do what you wanted to do. Imagine right now, if everyone...yes everyone...all at once could use those same few seconds and do what they wanted or needed to do. Our entire existence would most likely be altered forever. History would be changed. Things would be invented. Relationships would start or end. Crazy ideas would become regular coffeehouse talk. People would live longer because of a discovery. Someone would follow his or her own dreams because you followed yours.

When I was very young, I heard the life story of Helen Keller. I remember learning about how people who were blind had to learn differently, so they learned Braille. I found it fascinating to see how deaf people communicated by sign language. So when I heard the story of Helen Keller, who was both deaf and blind, I just couldn't understand how she ever overcame learning the basics of communication, let alone becoming a person who had a huge effect on society and history.

Helen Keller lost the ability to see and hear at nineteen months old. She grew up determined to communicate as conventionally as possible; with the help of her teacher, Anne Sullivan, she learned to speak, eventually spending much of her life as a lecturer. Keller was world-famous and is remembered as an advocate for people with disabilities, among her other causes. Keller wrote a total of twelve published books and on September 14, 1964, President Lyndon B. Johnson awarded her the Presidential Medal of Freedom, one of the United States' two highest civilian honors.

When I am reminded about courage like this, I think, "What is my excuse for not living my best life?"

Stepping into the ring can be scary and even paralyzing. For you to move out of your comfort zone and into the ring, you may have to do things you don't want to do. Some of these things might be the hardest things you have ever had to do.

Several years ago, I had to make a decision to step into the ring. For years, I had been trying to solve a situation of being attacked by continuous false allegations outside of the ring. I was pretty creative in attempting things outside of the ring to make the situation stop. Stepping into the ring meant fighting. I don't like conflict, but sometimes stepping into the ring is what is necessary. There are times when staying out of the ring can serve you, but not if you keep doing the same thing and getting the same disappointing result. I knew I had to step into the ring. This meant I had to step into the ring with the very people I wanted to avoid at all costs and file a lawsuit against the parties. Stepping into the ring provided different results than I experienced outside of the ring. I learned that it is the reason why you step into the ring that matters. It is about doing what is right, not what is nice. I had to learn those are two different things. Stepping into the ring was a test of my courage and faith. What ring or what fight or what cause do you know that you need to step into, but are avoiding?

There is a martial arts practice of breaking a board with the palm of your hand while someone else holds the board in front of you. I have done this myself and was surprised that by learning a few things, breaking the board was not as hard as I would have anticipated. Although technique is important, I found that technique alone usually wouldn't break the board. Let's look at breaking the board as the thing you don't want to do, but that you are going to force yourself to do. Here are the steps as published on WikiHow. com with some of my own notes added. (Mel was right; you can get information on how to do anything):

1. Choose your board. (Note: That's right; you have to make a choice.)

2. Secure the board—the best way is have a recruit who is at least your strength and weight hold the board for you. (Note: This sounds like an accountability partner for your project or obstacle. You don't have to do it alone.)

3. The break to start with is a palm strike at a 45-degree angle downwards, with the target board held at that 45-degree angle from horizontal at a little above waist height. This angle and position makes it easiest to put your bodyweight into the motion. Hit the board straight on with the heel of your hand. (Note: Hit it straight on! No shortcuts.)

4. The board should be held with the grain parallel to your fingers. If you hit it sideways, injury is exponentially more likely than success. (Note: Hit it straight on!)

5. Empty your mind. Relax. Don't think about success or failure. Take a calming breath. Focus yourself first. Unless you are extremely weak or sick (in which case you shouldn't be breaking boards at all), mental preparation is the most important aspect of the technique. (Note: Mental preparation is the most important aspect! Do not worry about the outcome; just focus on the thing you know you have to do.)

6. Now focus on the target. Breaking effectively is less about the amount of force you apply than about putting all that force at the single point of your choice. (Note: Focus on the one thing you know you need to do. We often worry about our strength or we dilute it by focusing on too many targets.)

7. Strike through the target. Don't aim at the board itself; if you do that, your hand will tend to stop there. Aim your strike six inches beyond the board. (Note: You most likely don't like looking at the thing you know you have to do, so you don't attempt it. Don't look at it! Look six inches beyond. What is there? Yes! The thing you are trying to gain is right there and you get it!)

8. Concentrate on speed, not power. You're not trying to push the board away; you're trying to hit it as fast as possible. (Note: Focus on that one point and make it count!)

9. Yell. The kiai that martial artists often emit when striking is

not just for show, nor to startle the opponent. The contraction of the diaphragm and torso muscles can be used to put more power in your strike. (Note: Through this process, find your voice and let other people know what it is. It will hold you accountable, but it will also inspire others when they hear and watch you.)

10. Give it your all. Commit your strike. Don't hesitate; don't think; just do it. (Note: Just do it! You can do it. I'm right here with you!)

11. Follow through. Don't try to stop your hand after the break; relax and let the motion end on its own. If you try to over-control, you will tense up and rob yourself of power. Mental knowledge is the key to a successful break. (Note: After the break, let it go and know that what you are trying to accomplish is right there and you can relax in it.)

12. If you do prepare mentally, and commit your strike fully, you will succeed. Even prepubescent children have the physical capacity to break boards; for any adult in reasonable health, all the obstacles are mental. (Note: You have what it takes! Isn't that amazing?)

Stepping into the ring for you may look more like sitting at a casino table with a pile of chips in front of you. You may have been playing a little bit and only at certain times, but you know you need to go all in. You know you have all the chips you need and you are one decision away from a totally different life. Just sitting at the table causes you anxiety because you know you have what it takes. Going all in is one of the trickiest maneuvers at the poker table, but it is what it is going to take. The decision is yours.

What if doing what you don't want to do right now allows you to do more of what you want long-term? What if stepping into the ring or going "all in" would allow you to live your life alive?

You will either conquer your fear or you will fail.

Exercise:

What ring do you need to step into or what table do you need to sit at so you can drastically move forward in life?

_____
_____
_____
_____
_____

What does the wood board signify in your life?

_____
_____
_____
_____
_____

Could you dedicate an exact time to step into the ring and commit, no matter what, to those few seconds it's going to take? What is the exact time you are going to do this? State the exact date and time.

_____
_____
_____
_____

What happens in your life when you choose to break the board?

_____
_____
_____
_____
_____
_____
_____
_____

Is the reward worth the effort or not?

_____
_____
_____
_____
_____
_____
_____
_____

How will you feel after those few seconds, regardless of the outcome?

_____
_____
_____
_____
_____
_____
_____

CHAPTER TEN

LIVE LIKE YOU'RE MOVING

"You are worth the fresh paint."

— Autumn Shields

Have you ever sold a house and discovered that the best your house ever looked was right before you moved out? Why did you wait and make it nice for someone else and not yourself?

I am aware of the saying, "Live like you're dying." The truth is we are all dying, but we usually don't go around acting like it. However, the other night I did throw on a dress to go out to dinner. I was overdressed, but I thought, "What if I'm not around tomorrow to wear it?" That was out of the norm. Do you go around acting like today is your last day? Probably not, so let's instead focus on living like we're moving.

Why is it that our house is always in the best shape when we are getting ready to move out or put it up for sale? Why do we tend to put off fixing, updating, or making things feel like our own? Maybe we know that the place is temporary, so why bother? I would like you to take a look around your surroundings and environment. What would you do if you had to move this week? Would you plant a garden, change a light fixture, put in a faucet that works, or even wash those windows so your view was better?

Do you like the place in which you live? Why do you live there? Why that dwelling, that neighborhood, and that city? What, inside or outside of your dwelling, makes you feel grounded and at home? What things do you have around you that inspire you daily? How does it feel to walk in the door? Do you feel like it sucks the air out of you, or does it feel like air fills you up as you walk inside. Do you avoid going home? Is the place too big or too small? Sometimes, we just live, but we don't stop to make our place worth living alive in. What would it feel like to spend some time and effort to make your home feel more like the place you desire?

I'm sure you are saying, "Well, if I had the time or money, my place would be a lot different." Everything happens in steps, remember? I'm not saying we need to jump into looking like a page out of *Better Homes and Gardens* magazine. Why not do what you can? Why wait until you are moving to paint that wall or fix those stairs? Take time to visualize what environment makes you feel cozy, creative, safe, and grounded. To live our life alive, we need to recognize what environment we feel good living in.

What about your work environment? What do you like? What would you change? What can you change? What type of environment do you work well in daily? Quiet, alone, with others, active, inside, outside? If we don't stop and identify this, how are we supposed to be our best and do our best? Get off the hamster wheel and think!

Have you found your tribe? You know, that group of friends who make you your best you and make you feel alive? If we don't think about this, we might be missing out on some great relationships. Have you found those people who inspire you or make you think more about what you like to think about? If you haven't, seek them out. Find places where people you like hang out, and be a friend to them first. Surrounding ourselves with others who appreciate us for who we are, and whom we can appreciate for their authentic selves, makes us feel better about ourselves. You are worth being in an environment where you feel valued and accepted. As for those people who don't accept you for you, that's okay. They are just on their own journeys. Bless and release them. Don't beat yourself up and try to fit in. Be yourself. Everyone else is taken. There are many people who are waiting to connect with you and take in what you have to offer.

When I moved away from my hometown to Maui, which is part of a chain of islands that is the most isolated landmass on the earth, I thought my relationships would suffer because I would be so far away. What I found to be true is that authentic connections are never lost by distance or by time apart. I have actually found that the relationships can become even stronger. It also gave me the space to look around and decide whom I wanted in my tribe. What kinds of people have similar attitudes about life? Who is different than me, but would enhance my life as I enhance theirs? People can make or break us. Find your tribe! With social media and many sites that connect people through interests, it's easier than ever.

When you make the decision to move, you tend to think of all the things you want to do before you leave the area. How does the amusement park, the museum, the ski slope, or the ballet sound? Why didn't you go last week or last month? You are worth it! You are worth getting out of your daily routine and making time to live your life alive. What are you spending your time doing?

When I was leaving Denver, I crammed a Broncos game, a Rockies game, all my favorite restaurants, salsa dancing, a birthday party/fundraiser, and going through twenty boxes of pictures into one week...and all the fun stuff that goes along with a normal move. What was I thinking? More importantly, what had I been doing? Now, when I go back to the place I lived for forty years, I cram in snowshoeing, skiing, rafting, games, and all of the things I only did once or twice previously in all the years I lived there. We all have tasks we have to tend to, such as work, kids' schedules, cleaning the house, and running the car in for an oil change, but we also need to fit in the things we want to do now. Don't wait until you are moving.

The reason it is so important for you to know you are worth the fresh paint and so much more is that if you feel "nudged" to do something, and it seems like that might be too good, or too exciting, or actually might be the answer you have been praying for, but you don't think you are worth it, you could miss or dismiss the nudge. The more you step into knowing you deserve to live your life alive, the more you will recognize and accept the nudges.

Exercises:

What one thing can you change about your living or work environment to make it feel like *your* space in the next seven days? Month? Year?

_____
_____
_____
_____
_____
_____
_____

If you moved to a place where you didn't know anyone, who would you like to connect with? Is that person similar to anyone you are close to now?

_____
_____
_____
_____
_____
_____

What kind of person do you enjoy being around?

_____
_____
_____
_____
_____
_____

Are you open to meeting more people who make you feel valued and accepted?

_____
_____
_____
_____
_____
_____
_____
_____

Who are the people in your life whom you can have real conversations with?

_____
_____
_____
_____
_____
_____

If you found out that you were moving, what activities would you want to do in your area?

_____
_____
_____
_____
_____
_____

Who are the people you would want to see and spend time with before you moved?

_____

_____

_____

_____

_____

_____

_____

_____

_____

_____

_____

_____

CHAPTER ELEVEN

SEEING IT THROUGH

"My legacy is that I stayed on course...from the beginning to the end, because I believed in something inside of me."
— Tina Turner

Have you ever left the movie theatre before the end of the movie? Have you ever broken up with someone because you felt he or she was going nowhere in life, and then the next thing you know, that person gets the job he or she has been waiting on for years while you believed he or she was just all talk? Have you ever quit a job because you couldn't stand the politics, but shortly after you left, the people who were causing the mayhem were all replaced?

When should we see things through? We can never tell for sure when the right time is to stay, when to walk away, or when to run! Hindsight is always 20/20.

We make mistakes along the way with our choices, but the one thing we cannot do is give up on ourselves. When we feel that nudge and we know we are meant for more, we cannot give up. When it seems humanly impossible, we have to have faith that there is a way. When we walk in faith, acting as if whatever we are waiting for has already happened, the path displays itself.

I'm going to share a few quick stories of times when I stayed and saw things through to the end and beyond. I call these sunset moments. I call them that because living on Maui, sunsets can become an important part of the day. I have thousands of photos. Staring at the sun is not good for your eyes, but I can't help it. I see people clear the beach when it becomes cloudy, literally five minutes before the sun sets for the day. They think they know how it is going to turn out. But within minutes, there is a break in the clouds right above the endless water; then the light shoots out and lights up the sky in the most breathtaking sunsets. The clouds allow the light to bounce off of them and reflect the vivid colors that make the display picture worthy.

But those other people left...right before the show. Why not wait the five minutes and just enjoy the air or watch the waves crash on shore? Why do we put so much emphasis on the exact time of the sunset and then walk away from it? As my son has pointed out, "Who cares about the sunset? The sky is always more colorful right afterwards." We make things the point and forget to enjoy the surrounding moments. We forget to enjoy the right before, the point, and the after...the moments.

Have you ever left a sporting event because there was "no way" the losing team was going to win and you didn't want to get stuck in traffic? You left before the victory. Or how about the time you were glued to your TV for hours and then you got bored and changed the station? You sat through the whole game and missed one of the best plays in sports. Then all you hear about for the next several days is how you missed one of the best comebacks of all time.

I've done this more than once. You would think I would learn to stay until the end. If you are going to watch, you might as well watch all of the plays. During the 2012 football season, being the Broncos fan that I am, I was watching the game at a friend's house. The Broncos were down 24-0 at halftime. Figuring I knew how the game would turn out, I decided to leave early. Meanwhile, the Broncos won 35-24. I missed the best plays of the game.

In 2001, the Cleveland Indians played the Seattle Mariners. The Indians were able to climb out of a twelve-run deficit against the Mariners. It all happened after the seventh inning, with the Tribe eventually winning the game 15-14 in eleven innings. Can you imagine watching the entire game, but it wasn't until the very end that there were thirteen more runs?

Think about how the following stories would have ended and how the world would be different if these companies hadn't stuck with it.

The name LEGO is an abbreviation of the Danish words "leg godt," meaning "play well." The Lego company says, "It's our name and it's our ideal." Since being founded in 1932, the Lego company has passed from father to son and its toys have remained favorites for generations of children—until the 1990s when the rise of video games and other competitors caused the company to start losing money for the first time. Then Jørgen Vig Knudstorp stepped in as CEO in 2004, and things started to "snap into place." Knudstorp cut costs and introduced new Lego lines like Ninjago that quickly became popular. The result: By 2013, Lego was the world's most profitable toymaker.

Apple is one of the most impressive business comebacks of the past twenty years. Founded in 1976, the giant began to flounder in the late '90s. Then Steve Jobs resurrected it so that today it is the most valuable company in the world.

In my own story, as I built a network marketing business and started promoting to the first few levels, I was told I should dress like a VP, act like a VP, and introduce myself as a VP. I thought, "That is ridiculous! Those things are earned." I would not introduce myself as something I was not. I would hear other people say, "Fake it until you make it!" I thought, "I'm not faking anything!" I was told, "When you drive around, imagine being in the car you earned." I would think, "I'm just fine in my car. I'm never going to earn a car from my company."

I thought a lot of things that aren't compatible with having a winner's brain. I thought I wasn't worthy. I thought money was evil. I thought only people who looked a certain way were successful. I thought people had to have a title to lead. I thought no one was going to follow me when I was broke and living in an apartment. I was wrong. International speaker Rita Davenport would tell us, "Mind your mind. This business is between your ears." I struggled with the negative thoughts going on between my ears, but I did the work I needed to do. Within a year, I was promoted to a VP position in my company. I never thought I could reach even the first level. But others believed I could do it. I leaned on their belief. I also leaned on others who went ahead of me and I borrowed their belief. If nothing else, I proved others and maybe even myself wrong! When you set out to follow your dream, give others a good show! People are watching you. If you say you are going to do something, do it. Be a person of your word. Your actions will inspire others.

Set realistic expectations about your ideas and goals. We live in a "microwave" culture and expect everything to happen very quickly. Most of the time, things happen in a much more "Crockpot" fashion. If we let them cook slow and steady, they will get done and done well. Just don't quit before payday!

I encourage you to have good, great, and awesome goals, and not to give up on them.

I have a good friend, Joe Kapushion, say to me, "I always have really high goals and low expectations." I thought to myself, *Low expectations are not a very positive outlook*. He continued to explain, "Then whatever happens usually falls somewhere in between and there is no disappointment. If there is no disappointment, you have the tendency to feel more satisfied and keep moving forward." Joe has found a lot of success by falling in between high goals and low expectations.

A trap that you can easily fall into is the trap of expectations projected into the future. For example, if you have high expectations for how a date is going to go with your partner, or for your next business meeting, or your child coming home and doing chores and homework without being reminded, or how dinner is going to taste, you are simply projecting expectations into the future. It is impossible to stay present in the moment and let the small, yet important moments happen. If you tend to get disappointed in people or the situation, it is usually because you saw something different happening. I am not suggesting that you don't visualize what you want and set goals or targets. I am a huge proponent of visualization. I am, however, suggesting that you lay down all projected expectations and live in the moment. Practice on simple things, such as food. If I look at something and say, "That is a brownie and brownies are my favorite," I may have a certain expectation for how a brownie should taste. Then if I taste it and am disappointed, that is because of my expectations. Instead, I could say, "I wonder what this tastes like," and be present and open to what it has to offer. What about bigger things, such as time with your partner or children? Do you see how a day looks before it even exists? Do you get upset with your partner because you thought he or she would act differently during that place in time and miss something amazing that he or she did do? Are you disappointed in your children because you expected a certain situation to play out differently than it did? You can't control other people! So why not try visualizing yourself being present in the moment? What if your projected expectations are actually limiting how much better it could be? Catch the miracles in the moments! You can live a lot more alive when you keep expectations low and your goals high and you are willing to play life in between. What happens might just surprise you! What you may experience are things beyond your limited thinking or even beyond your wildest imagination!

Rather than focusing on your expectations for the future, try to be present in the moment and act in the moment with a positive attitude. People often wait for the outcome to evaluate how they did or how they should feel. You can feel great by just doing an activity and serving what you are called to do. The results will come. You can always use the term "unbelievable" when asked how that "thing" you are working on is going! No one needs to know whether it is going unbelievably good or bad.

"What is the difference between an obstacle and an opportunity? Our attitude toward it. Every opportunity has a difficulty, and every difficulty has an opportunity."

— J. Sidlow Baxter

Stay the course! Don't leave before the sun sets. Don't leave before payday.

I challenge you to see it through. You are worth it!

People are watching. Give them a good show! See it through.

Exercise:

What have you quit and not seen through?

_____
_____
_____
_____
_____
_____

What do you think it cost you?

_____
_____
_____
_____
_____
_____
_____
_____

What have you done all the way through that allowed you to experience the rewards?

_____
_____
_____
_____
_____
_____
_____

Is there an area or areas where you could adjust your attitude? Perhaps toward expectations, time, people, or yourself?

_____
_____
_____
_____
_____
_____
_____

What kind of show are you showing yourself and the world?

_____
_____
_____
_____
_____

What will you commit to today that you will see through?

_____
_____
_____
_____
_____

What will it cost you if you don't see it through?

_____
_____
_____
_____
_____

What will you gain or earn if you do see it through?

_____
_____
_____
_____
_____
_____
_____

CHAPTER TWELVE

LOVING UNTIL IT HURTS

"Let our scars fall in love."

— Galway Kinnell

Isn't love grand? How can we talk about living alive and not visit the "L" word. Loving until it hurts can be seen as the same concept as living to the point of tears. It is just a matter of depth.

Have you ever felt love or been in love? Have you received unconditional love from a family member or given it to another?

I have been writing about love in the form of love poems and letters since about the age of nine. I'm a hopeless romantic. I believe love makes the world go 'round and love is the answer to all things.

Numerous studies have shown that love is not just a good feeling we get, but that it is actually good for us. And not just romantic love, but all kinds of love. Many studies show that we just need more love to have better health and an overall better life.

If you are in a good place with loving relationships, I bet you are saying, "Well, yes, love is awesome." If you are not, I can hear you grumbling and doubting. If you have loved and lost someone, I can hear the pain through your thoughts.

We all want to feel love and want to give love. So let's address a few things that might be holding you back from feeling love.

The first thing that often holds people back is hanging on to offenses. Yes, if people have offended you, hurt you, taken from you, mistreated you, you have to let it go. You don't have to forget, but letting go is necessary.

A goal to living your life alive is to try not to be offended. Imagine that! Not only letting go of past offenses but learning not to take offense in the first place.

I heard a sermon once on the topic of offenses that provided a great analogy on what happens when we hold on and gather offenses. Let's say that when someone does something to offend you, it is like that person picked up a rock and threw it at you. The offense is real! But you have some choices to make. You can try to move out of the way and let the rock land somewhere else. You can let the rock hit you and then land on the ground. You can catch the rock and carry it around. Or you can take the rock and stack it on the wall of other rocks you have caught in the past.

We all get offenses thrown at us, and those rocks come in all shapes and sizes. But what we do with those offenses can hold us back from living alive. If you can avoid getting hit, great! Why stand in the way? If you can move, move! Sometimes, you know how a situation is going to turn out but you stand there anyway. Just move.

Or if you do get hit, what if you just let it fall to the ground? Sometimes, even though you get hit, it has nothing to do with you. Don't take it personally.

If you catch the rock, you are taking ownership, and that means that any rock you catch adds a weight that you have to carry around. Sometimes you carry it around and show it to others. "Look what he did to me! Or can you believe she did this to me?" Whom does that serve? People know the offense is real and the rock was thrown. Showing the offense over and over just gives it more power and takes your power away.

Lastly, if you catch the rock and place it on the wall of other rocks, you can stay safely behind it. However, this is the worst place to be if you want to live alive. Living alive allows your light to shine. No one can see you shine from behind the wall. People may get small glimpses of your light shining through the spaces between the rocks, but the world needs your whole light. You might even allow a few people to come visit you behind the wall, but visitation is just a substitute for real connection.

How is your rock situation?

President Abraham Lincoln said, "We should be too big to take offense and too noble to give it."

Anger gets a hold of you and tries to hang on for the ride. Gautama

Buddha warns, "Holding onto anger is like drinking poison and expecting the other person to die." Anger does not serve love or you, so let it go.

Chasing the wrong thing or the wrong someone could also be holding you back. Lolly Daska, president and CEO of Lead From Within, a global consultancy firm that specializes in leadership and entrepreneurial development, says, "When you stop chasing the wrong things, you give the right things a chance to catch you." Sometimes, we are so desperate to find love that we accept average, or we accept good instead of striving for great. Don't settle! You are worth great. If someone is taking more air out of you than putting it into you, that person is probably not serving you or him- or herself.

Past rejection could be causing you fear. Rejection is never fun. In my early twenties, a girlfriend and I were sitting with one of our male friends, Reese Lee, discussing whether we thought a certain guy was going to call my friend back. He said he was going to be calling that weekend, but she hadn't heard from him. Reese, said, "If someone wants to be with you, they just will be." It really is that simple. Nobody likes rejection, but spending your energy on people who are interested is so much more rewarding.

Rejection can be even more painful and limiting if it comes from someone with whom we had a relationship. A past lost that caused major pain could be holding us back.

When we do experience the loss of a relationship, it can cause us grief, but we can't remain there. If you need to, get help, from friends or counseling, or whatever is necessary. But don't give up on love.

Rebuild so you can live your life alive. Maybe many of your dreams were tied in with the person you lost. You can still dream, and you can find someone else to share new dreams with. Dreaming is free. So why not start dreaming or keep on dreaming? You are worth love. Give love a bigger chance than you give fear. I chose to commit to love over fear. I figured you can get a lot more out of love than fear. After my first divorce and learning that people who say they love you can actually spend an enormous amount of time and energy hurting you, I still decided to give love another chance. However, I was terrified to trust again, and I didn't want to mess up and make a poor decision again. My mom said, "You can get married again; just don't marry another cop." I married another cop. He was the love of my life and I was able to spend almost ten years with him and his children. It was a blessing. Although I was heartbroken, I had to realize that I couldn't give in to fear. I chose to surrender to love and all that has it has to offer...the good and the bad.

To love, sometimes you have to forgive. It is impossible to live your life alive when you are bound by what someone else chose to do. Forgiveness is not about letting the other person off the hook; it's about letting yourself off the hook. I chose love. Most importantly, I chose to love myself.

There is a Jewish blessing that I think is great. It is: Strive to treat each other as if it's your first day together, your last day together, and your only day together. Imagine if we followed this how so many of our relationships would change or how we experience them would be different. Today matters. Love deeply and celebrate all the love in your life.

Exercise:

Is there an offense, or offenses, that you are holding onto and using to build a wall?

_____
_____
_____
_____
_____

Is there someone you can forgive to let yourself off the hook?

_____
_____
_____
_____
_____
_____

Is there a dream you need to let go of so you can start dreaming a different dream?

_____
_____
_____
_____
_____
_____

What love do you currently have in your life that you can celebrate?

_____

_____

_____

_____

_____

_____

Whom can you reach out to today, and what can you do to show that person your love?

_____

_____

_____

_____

_____

_____

CHAPTER THIRTEEN

LIFE-CHANGING MOMENTS

"It is in your moments of decision that your destiny is shaped."

— Tony Robbins

C an you identify the moments that changed the course of your life? Or those moments that stirred something inside of you and there was a shift?

Maybe you made a decision. Perhaps someone made it for you. Maybe it was a traumatic event that changed the course of your life. Maybe you had prepared for one thing and something else happened that changed your path. The moments I want you to look at here are the moments that were about your life and living it alive. Maybe it was a nudge that just seemed to come out of nowhere. Maybe it was the thing stirring inside of you that you just had to do, but you didn't know how or if it would work. It can be important to reflect on these moments in your past and be open to them in the future.

Gregg Walker is a senior vice president for Sony Corporation of America and is noted as one of the most powerful African-Americans in the nation under forty. He believes in facing fears and challenging himself. In 2010, on his thirty-eighth birthday, he set a goal that had nothing to do with the boardroom or Sony's bottom line—something completely outside his comfort zone. Walker vowed he would tackle stand-up comedy.

What would it be like to stand in front of an audience of people whose mood would decide your future? Okay, for Walker, it wasn't really his future. He was still rich and powerful, but the fear of failure was still real.

Walker spent time writing jokes and attending afternoon practice runs with other comedians. His business experience ended up working well on stage. Other comics kept telling him his style was like a board presentation. Most didn't know he was an executive. He saw the comments as a bad sign, but his new friends told him his style was unique—they thought it would work.

Walker's debut came with a sense of relief. He had been nervous as he worked to develop his act, but once the show drew near, he felt relief. "It was going to be over soon," he said about his fear of failing.

At the time of Walker's comic debut, Tiger Woods' sex scandal was in the news; Walker happens to look very much like a younger version of Woods. He stepped on stage and said, "Tiger Woods is nervous about going back to golf...."

The audience laughed.

"I'm nervous about Tiger Woods going back to golf...."

The crowd laughed more.

Walker hadn't even made it to the punch line and the crowd was already rolling.

"I learned from my corporate world how to get up there and talk and not let the fear overtake you," Walker said. "I learned from comedy that most of us use too much set-up and not enough punch line. We can all work on whittling down the set-up."

We spend too much time on the set-up. We can't live alive in the set-up. Cut to the punch line. Take the chance. Listen to the nudge.

Four major life-changing moments have shaped where I am today. Of course, the choice of marriage and children was obvious; however, the life-changing moments listed below seemed to come out of nowhere. I felt the nudge. These were major nudges. I have now learned to identify the very small, quiet nudges, but these were the big ones.

The first one happened when I was in eighth grade. I received a call from one of my friends who told me one of our classmates had committed suicide. The news shook my world; it was the first time I realized people might want to hurt themselves or end their own lives. It was a weird concept for a thirteen-year-old girl to understand. When I received more information, I decided I needed to go tell other people about it face-to-face. My day consisted of knocking on doors and getting classmates together. This was the start of my career, but I didn't realize it at the time. I did know my life had been completely changed.

To help answer our questions, a meeting at a neighborhood home was arranged by the local police department. A woman named Susan, with the title of victim advocate, spoke to us, introducing some support tools we could use to help each other and ourselves to cope with our grief. I didn't understand this woman's job except that she worked for the police department.

During the next year at school, as a freshman, I joined the peer counseling team. One of our assignments was to find someone in the field whom we could shadow. I met with and interviewed the victim advocate, Susan, who had spoken at the neighborhood meeting. What she told me changed the course of my life. When I asked her how she had chosen her career, she told me: 1). She wanted to do something that was the same job but different every single day. 2). She wanted to help people in a police, counseling, and/or court setting but did not want to be a police officer, therapist, or attorney. 3). She had kept looking for this job, even though she didn't know its title. Then she told me the educational requirements and said if I ever needed her, she would be there for me. She said she believed in me.

Not everyone has to agree with your decisions or choices. They are yours. I decided to go for it. I am walking proof that if one person believes in you, you can accomplish your goals.

The next moment was when I was nudged to leave my career and build my own business. I had no business being in business. Honestly, at the time, I barely had time to shower. Who was I to start a business? I was working full-time and working a "little gig" on the side, but when I felt the nudge to make the jump, I felt pure panic and immediately I resisted. I remember actually feeling like I was digging my heels in the ground and saying, "No way."

My next life-changing moment came in early January of 2012 while visiting Maui, Hawaii. I was on an incentive trip, which I had earned as an independent consultant, from a network marketing company. Early one morning, I was walking the beach. The breeze was crisp and the ocean was tinted pink from the early morning sun kissing it. I sat in a great spot, near a place called Black Rock, and took out my notebook, which I had brought along so I could reflect on the prior year, record my goals for the coming year, and write out a plan to accomplish those goals. As I started to write, I felt uneasy and uncomfortable. I even felt a little annoyed, which is unusual. I couldn't get comfortable. I couldn't get my mind to focus on the task at hand. At the resort the day prior, I was supposed to take a fitness class, but there was a mistake on the schedule, so it ended up being a meditation class. I had never meditated before, and it wasn't that great of a class; however, the instructor did teach me how to set thoughts aside and just "be." So I tried my newly learned technique. I sat facing the sea with my eyes closed and took deep breaths. This only proved more agitating.

Finally, after much internal resistance, I laid down on the sand with my palms up. I once again tried to set my thoughts aside. Deep breaths. I simply said out loud, "I surrender." I felt a huge rush of

141

peace come over me. I couldn't move. The nudge wasn't just a little nudge as a suggestion. It was more like a harsh download of information. Time seemed to stand still. Tears ran down my face onto the sand. I felt whole and totally connected to the earth. I felt the nudge to serve that piece of earth. A little rock, called Maui, sitting in the middle of the Pacific. Time passed. Then I got up and wrote and wrote in my notebook. On the pages appeared an outline for a non-profit to serve children and a for-profit business involving cultural exchange with ocean/land experiences with visitors. I thought I could actually move to Maui...someday.

The most recent nudge was this book. By now, you would think I would be more aware and more obedient to my nudges. But I dismissed it. It took several people saying something to me intentionally or random encounters that included someone encouraging me to write. Even my ex-husband, Philip, called out of the blue and said, "I have something for you." We met and he handed me a book about how to write a book. This was several years ago. He told me I had a story I was going to write. I thought about it and concluded it was a weird encounter. I put the idea on the shelf, probably because this nudge didn't seem to align with any desire at the forefront of my life. I knew it would be work, but what I wanted was rest.

Are you experiencing life-changing moments, or is life just happening to you?

Exercise:

What is your timeframe for bringing what is important to you to fruition?

_____
_____
_____
_____
_____
_____
_____

Honestly, what is your attitude toward what is in front of you that you would like to accomplish?

_____
_____
_____
_____
_____
_____
_____
_____
_____
_____

What safety nets or accountability could you put in place to help you see it through?

_____
_____
_____
_____
_____
_____
_____

CHAPTER FOURTEEN

OBEYING THE NUDGE

"Our deepest fear is that we are powerful beyond measure. It is our light, not our darkness that most frightens us. We ask ourselves, who am I to be brilliant, gorgeous, talented, fabulous? Actually, who are you not to be? You are a child of God. Your playing small does not serve the world. There is nothing enlightened about shrinking so that other people won't feel insecure around you. We are all meant to shine, as children do. We were born to make manifest the glory of God that is within us. It's not just in some of us; it's in everyone. And as we let our own light shine, we unconsciously give other people permission to do the same. As we are liberated from our own fear, our presence automatically liberates others."

— Marianne Williamson

So what happened when I obeyed the nudges?

As I followed the path through high school and college, I stayed focused on what I knew I was supposed to do. There were many distractions along the way, but anytime I even glanced the other way, I would feel the nudge to stay on track. My parents even offered to pay for me to go to travel school so I could see the world. Travel is my passion, but I chose to follow the nudge. I knew it wasn't about me.

I interviewed for a job I was under-qualified for, and while I was walking in, I prayed, "I surrender. Use me as an instrument." I was hired and became the youngest advocate in the field at the time. I called Susan, the advocate who was my mentor in high school, and said, "Hi, Susan. This is Autumn Shields. I just wanted to let you know I am the new advocate serving the city that borders yours. I want to thank you for guiding me and believing in me."

The next time I obeyed a nudge was more difficult. I had followed my first nudge and jumped into a career. Although I had to stay focused, it was my first calling and it led to a career I was passionate about. We have skills and desires that are meant to be fulfilled because many times it is not about us. However, this next nudge to start my own business seemed a little uninteresting compared to what I was currently doing—in fact, it actually seemed absurd. Somehow I found the time to open my mouth and refer products that were working for me. As with any referral that I give, I never expected to receive anything from it. I didn't understand that the company was referral marketing and that I would benefit from just sharing what I loved. Actually, as I mentioned earlier, when I received my first check for referring a friend, I called the company and told it I didn't want a check and I didn't want to be involved in this type of business. Once I got over my big fat ego and opened myself to learning more about the industry, things shifted. I was open to the idea of supplementing my family's income. I had decided to work my business part-time to make a little extra money and stay focused on my career. My career was what I was called to do, and I was doing it.

Then it happened! I felt the nudge. I started hearing that I needed to make this little thing big and go all in. All in? What? And give up security and what I was called to do? I had a thirty-year plan I was on. I struggled and fought, but I kept seeing signs that I needed to jump. Ten months later, I was making more at this cute part-time gig than I was in my full-time job answering calls about sexual assault and domestic violence. I started dreaming again and realizing that while I was loving my job, I wasn't living my life. I even announced that I would soon be leaving my career in law enforcement before I had an increase of income in my personal business. Almost every morning, my son and I would play and sing at the top of our lungs Janis Joplin's song, "Mercedes Benz." It is the car that you get as a bonus when you are promoted to the VP level. Even though my actions showed belief, I still had some doubt. I couldn't worry about the doubt. I had to focus on my belief. A year after I committed to working my business intentionally in the nooks and crannies of my busy life, I was promoted to a VP level. I was able to wake up and start to live a life by design. I didn't know exactly what I was getting myself into, but I thought, "I'm sure going to find out!" What would you have done?

When I felt the nudge to move to Maui, I happened to be bound, in Colorado, by a custody order, that prevented my son from leaving the state because his father had visitation rights. This was in place for four more years. I returned home and shared the idea with my fourteen-year-old son. He said, "Let's go." I explained to him that there was a court order in place, but we could plan now to move later. Immediately, he called me on my faith, and said, "If this is really a true calling, why would you think the court order is bigger or more powerful than the calling?" To myself I was thinking, "How sweet and childlike his faith is. He just doesn't understand the details of our reality."

Reality...ha! Who even knows what true reality is? I did have a plan. My plan was that I was going to go help girls in the sex slave industry in Thailand. It had been an interest of mine for years as a victim advocate, and it pulled at my heartstrings. I knew I could make a difference. This nudge moved me in a different direction. What if I held on tight to my plan? It wasn't a bad plan, right?

I have learned to follow the nudge. My understanding falls short, but my experience tells me that it is about the ripple effect.

Between the court order and the nudge saying, "Go now," the dates didn't match up, but that was not for me to worry about. They say when others see you coming, they will move out of your way. I had to move to get others to move. Are you waiting for others to move before you move?

I announced my intentions to my partner, my family, friends, and business associates. Can you imagine telling everyone you're moving and seeing the changes in your relationships immediately, only to have the judge say you're not going anywhere? I actually tried to hire one of the best trial attorneys in Denver. Her response was: "You're going to get your ass kicked in court. It would be unfair for me to take your money."

I also started selling our belongings. I bought Hawaiian music CDs and didn't listen to anything else in the car. I put apps on my phone that tied me to that area such as local news and weather alerts, and I learned a Hawaiian word a day. I started searching for schools and housing in the area. I booked a trip with my son a few weeks after I decided and we circled the island with prayer. The book *The Circle Maker* by Mark Batterson inspired this trip. He encourages you to physically circle what you are praying about. This is inspired by a story of a Jewish scholar by the name of Honi. During a severe drought, in the first century B.C., Honi drew a circle in the dirt and stood in the circle. He prayed, "Lord of the universe, I swear before Your great name that I will not move from this circle until you have shown mercy upon Your children." As it started to rain, he continued to pray for even more rain. The legend of Honi, the circle-maker, prayed what was considered to be one of the most significant prayers. The circle he drew became a sacred symbol. He showed the world what it was really like to draw a line in the sand. I had read it a month earlier and it was the gateway for me to start believing in things I didn't understand. It encouraged me to have audacious faith. As we circled the island, we started playing the imagine game: "Imagine if we lived in that neighborhood. Imagine if we could go to that beach. Imagine if we could eat dinner there." We didn't just imagine it; we did it.

I filed the motion to relocate a minor child on my own. I didn't even organize the usual amount of crazy paperwork, from boxes to binders, that documented the last decade and half of our lives. I had an almost paralyzing peace come over me the night before and the next day as I entered the courtroom. During the court proceedings, I asked the judge several times to talk to my thirteen-year-old son. Before court, I had already explained to my son that judges just don't talk to kids without them having individual representation or a child advocate involved, but I promised I would ask. As I continued to ask through the proceeding, it was reiterated that minors were not permitted to testify. An hour into proceedings, the courtroom was cleared and my son was asked to enter the large district courtroom by himself. An hour and ten minutes passed, which seemed like an eternity. My son just wanted his day in court. He wanted his voice heard. All he knew was that all of this court "stuff" went on between adults, but he never got a chance to be heard, without the interference from his parents. I knew he would be respectful toward both of his parents, and after all, it was his life. As he walked out of the courtroom, we sat on the stairs of the courthouse, and he broke down and cried. In front of me, I saw this young broken spirit, but I also saw a huge weight had been lifted from his shoulders because he was heard. He told me he was embarrassed because he cried in court. He had asked the judge, after he was able to say what he wanted to say and ask the questions he wanted to ask, whether he could shake his hand to say thank you for listening to him. On his way up to the bench, he started to cry. Without discussing or knowing the details about the testimony, I told my son, "Regardless of the outcome or if we get to move, I have never been more proud of you than I am today. You recognize you have a voice and you had the courage to use it today. Not only that, but to ask a judge to shake his hand, that shows your character." I continued to explain that many people never recognize or use their voice, and for that, I was so proud of him. He said, "Mom, I told you to have faith."

Once I decided to step out in faith, signs started appearing everywhere. I started meeting people who live in Maui. I had a friend who visited Maui and told me about this place called Kihei. My friend told me I should consider it as a place to land on Maui. That night when I went to another friend's house, I saw Kihei highlighted on the Travel Channel.

I could go on and on, but I won't. The only thing I would encourage you to do is have fun with the signs. Playing with it all is so much fun. If you stress about the details, you miss the fun. Before I moved or even knew I was moving, I started learning how to just be and surrender. One day, I was lying on my bed listening to a podcast on activating your own energy when I had a vision that actually caused me to sit straight up in bed to catch my breath. I had a vision that I was flying in the sky with other birds over one of the windiest harbors in the world. It was Maalaea Harbor. It was Maui. As the wind rushed by me, I felt the most amazing peace I had ever felt in my life. I knew right then it was done. Regardless of the things hindering the move, it was going to happen.

During this time, I had opened up like never before. I was open to things I couldn't understand or explain because I couldn't dismiss or deny them. I could feel things I had never felt before. I encountered people who popped into my life at the craziest of all places and strangest times. I am not sure how to categorize these people, and I don't want to label them with a specific term or title. These interactions seemed "supernatural."

A woman, Amy, who was giving me Reiki and providing me nutritional counseling, told me before I went to Maui, on the company trip, that something really big and life-changing was going to happen during my trip. She told me I was going to be scared initially and think it wasn't possible, but I would not be alone, and I would be okay. She told me I was going to find my voice again. I thought she was talking about business, not an entire life change. Later, I recognized she is one of those people whom I thought had one role in my life, but it turned out she also guided me in another way.

I had a very special friend, Luis, come into my life, that I met salsa dancing. Although he was a good dancer, he also ended up being one of those ordinary people whom I thought had one role but ended up serving as a guide. He would say things to me and understand things about me that he had no prior knowledge of. He would say these things out of the blue. I'm not kidding! It's not like we lit candles and tried to find answers with a Ouija board or we recited a specific prayer. He would literally be laughing about a fart that he just got done sharing with the world and then turn and say something with a different tone that would stop me in my tracks. He would call me out on my faith when I would question it. He would say things and pray in Spanish over me, and I would be moved like never before. That was when I realized that energy and love have no boundaries with people and that people can be guides to each other. I couldn't understand a word he was saying at times, but my life was forever changed. He not only believed in me and supported this transition in my life, but he was willing to be used as an instrument and just share his understanding and love. Luis would actually not recall these "happenings," or if he did, he would recall them in a casual manner. He would say that such things had happened to him since he was little so they were really no big deal. It wasn't a big deal to him, but it was to me. Things were said that gave me the comfort of knowing things had already been decided and I was moving.

Another time, I ran into a convenience store, which I hadn't done since gas pumps started accepting debit cards. I met a man, Jorge, who worked there and whom I quickly dismissed because I was in a hurry as usual. He came out and knocked on the window of my car. I was startled. He quickly explained that he was just trying to help me (I did not need help), and he gave me his card. It turned out he was a counselor and worked at a high school. However, he had felt nudged that summer to work at a gas station and meet people who were in need of his services. Again, I dismissed him and needed to go. He handed me his card and said, "Autumn, there is a joy missing in you that we need to talk about. The cloud that has been hanging over your head will soon be gone." I thought, "How did he know that?"

We met. He met my son and asked to speak to him alone. Afterwards, my son said, "Mom, I have no idea who that guy was, but I think he was an angel...weird." We never saw him again.

Not long after, as I was moving the last few boxes from my mother's car to take into her house to store, a picture fell out on the ground. All of my childhood pictures were in albums, but I was slacking as a mom and had many boxes of pictures of my own child's life that still needed to find a home in an album someday. I went to grab the picture off the ground, expecting it to be a cute little curly blond-haired kid. It was my grandmother. It was my grandmother on Maui. It was my grandmother standing in the exact spot on which I had had the vision. She was alone, standing and looking out to sea. I stood and cried. How could this be? Although we had visited Maui together at times, we had never visited that spot. Although she had passed, I knew she was with me all along.

153

A few months later, as we were landing on Maui, my son looked out the window of the plane and said, "Look, Mom; we're home."

Later, lying on the beach, I looked up and saw color like I had never seen before. At that moment, I knew I was free and living my life alive. I can feel love again, and I am in love again. I can unmask my face and adore it. I can sing and dance and laugh! And I have just begun!

I kept this unwritten book on the shelf for years. Sometimes, the right time is needed. Never wait to wait, but trust the timing. I did need rest, and I needed to start living my own life even more alive. It's what time, a decision, and Maui provided that for me. The entire time the unwritten book was on the shelf, I was aware it was there, and I honored it. I trusted the resources would appear. They always do if it's truly a nudge.

The resources appeared. I called to rent a Jeep from a private party for a friend coming to the island, and by chance, or more likely by divine intervention, the man who rented cars referred me to his neighbor who had a Jeep. I ended up on the phone with the guy who owned a Jeep, and he turned out to be an author, publishing coach, and professional speaker. We spoke and connected. Although I never rented his Jeep, a year later, he messaged me and said that he had woken up with the feeling that he needed to reach out to me. He was hosting a luncheon to help authors publish their books and was wondering whether I was writing a book. I told him, "I had just started attending a writing group a few months ago and I feel like the time is now." He replied, "I can help you."

The resources appeared. More importantly, what if he didn't follow the feeling he'd had and hadn't reached out to me? It wasn't about him; that feeling was about me. I wonder how many times I had a feeling to reach out to someone I could help and how many times I failed to do so. Thank goodness he did.

Are these experiences coincidences or meant to be? I had another man, Paul, walk right up to me while we were watching a Broncos game at a local hangout. He happened to know a lot about my company, and he just happened to be an author. We met later that week, at a coffee shop, and he encouraged me to use my voice. I recognized it right away. He was one of those ordinary people who is also a guide. He told me everything was stuck in my throat and it needed to come out. Weird! He asked whether we could walk to the park. He told me to breathe and close my eyes. I saw everything clearly. He had popped into my life and said the right thing at the right time, never being informed of my happenings. If there is that feeling that you can't shake and things just keep happening to keep nudging you along, I will tell you that it is meant to be.

There is one common thread that happened in all of these situations. I secured the nudge. What I mean by that is that I believed 110 percent that the nudge was God nudging me and not just a good idea. I knew the purpose was bigger than me. I knew the resources would appear. There is a big difference between expectations, goals, and nudges. But when you identify a nudge, you must listen and follow through with it. I learned in all of these situations that fear would rear its head, there would be dream stealers, and I would want to throw in the towel at times. So what I did, and I believe to be essential in following all the way through, is to secure the nudge. I made the announcement. I bought the outfit for the occasion. I sent out "hold the date" cards. I sold things. I listened to certain songs. I would spend time house hunting. I went and test drove a Mercedes. I started learning words in the Hawaiian language. I would go to writing groups and tell people I was writing a book before I started. I started selling this book before it was completed. I had to secure things so I couldn't back out. I put money down on a place to have a book release party before the book was done. It was easier for me to stay committed to the work then to have to re-buy all the furniture I had sold, and stay in the same house or return people's money from a book that never happened. I walked in faith and acted in faith. I can't even begin to explain how exhilarating the journey was with these experiences.

I can't even imagine the nudges I have missed so far. I'm sure I have dismissed nudges by thinking they were silly or impossible. I am sure I missed nudges because I wasn't present in the moment. I'm sure I have missed nudges because I wasn't open to them. Learning to "just be" has definitely helped me catch more nudges. They are everywhere! I can't even imagine the love I have missed so far by dismissing people because I was in a hurry, because I didn't know their intent and never gave them a chance to show me it was simply support or love. Look up from your phone and say hello to the next person you meet. Be open to love. Be open to support.

Surrendering to a Higher Power and being open to being used as an instrument is the place where authentic and divine works can do their job. This is where the road you can't see or understand is a pathway to changing things or people you may not even be aware of in this moment. There are hundreds, if not thousands of other good ideas I have had about my life and business. There is definitely a difference between a God idea and a good idea.

Seeing something through is about faith, patience, and attitude. Do you have the patience to see your ideas through? Do you have a realistic expectation of the timeframe? Do you have faith in a positive outcome?

One act of obeying the nudge will change your life.

Exercise:

List any prior nudges you have followed:

1. _____
2. _____
3. _____
4. _____
5. _____
6. _____
7. _____
8. _____
9. _____
10. _____
11. _____
12. _____
13. _____

What was the outcome/effect of following them?

_____

_____

_____

_____

_____

_____

_____

_____

Can you identify any nudges you dismissed?

_____

_____

_____

_____

_____

_____

_____

If you feel like there could be prior nudges you missed, what do you believe stopped you from following them?

_____

_____

_____

_____

_____

_____

_____

CHAPTER FIFTEEN

CREATING VISION FOR YOUR LIFE

"Men must live and create. Live to the point of tears."

— Albert Camus

D o you have a clear vision for your life?

I think actor Matthew McConaughey has a good handle on a life vision. In his 2014 Academy Award acceptance speech, after he listed the things he most needed in his life, including God and his family, he concluded with "someone to chase," about which he said:

> [M]y hero, that's who I chase. Now, when I was fifteen years old, I had a very important person in my life come to me and say, "Who's your hero?" And I said, "I don't know, I've got to think about that. Give me a couple of weeks." I come back two weeks later, this person comes up and says, "Who's your hero?"...I said, "I thought about it. It's me in ten years." So I

turned twenty-five. Ten years later, that same person comes to me and says, "So, are you a hero?" And I was like, "Not even close! No, no, no!" She said, "Why?" I said, "Because my hero's me at thirty-five."

So, you see, every day, every week, every month, and every year of my life, my hero's always ten years away. I'm never going to be my hero. I'm not going to attain that. I know I'm not. And that's just fine with me, because that keeps me with somebody to keep on chasing. So, to any of us, whatever those things are, whatever it is we look up to, whatever it is we look forward to, and whoever it is we're chasing. To that I say: Amen. To that I say, All right, all right, all right. To that I say, just keep living, eh? Thank you.

What gives you energy when you are doing a task, versus sucking energy out of you? What makes you pound your fist on the table when the topic comes up because you are passionate about it? What tugs at your heart when you hear about it? What comes naturally to you and doesn't even feel like work to you?

Do you feel lost as to what you are good at or what your purpose is? Do you feel inadequate at many things? Are you smart? We are all smart in different ways. It is important to recognize and know your "smarts" so you know what you are good at and grow those areas. The following is a list of "smarts." The definitions are general, and you do not need to meet every part of the definition to be that "smart." I was first introduced to the Smarts when volunteering for a mentoring program, "Making Choices," sponsored by the Center for Spirituality at Work. Making Choices teaches decision-making and life-planning skills to women incarcerated at Denver Women's Correctional Facility. I was taught by a brilliant woman by the name of Dr. Vie Thorgren. Dr. Thorgren taught us to help others identify their strengths and values, and from learning about those people, we can make good decisions. These teachings can be used by any of us. The first nine "smarts" listed I learned from the program. The other thirteen were identified by the youth I work with in The Makoa Project on Maui.

The Smarts:

> **Physical Smart:** You learn best by doing something hands on; you want to get personal, physical contact with the subject; you feel a need to move while you're learning; your favorite pastimes probably involve activities or handiwork; you have an ability to manipulate things with your hands or to dance or move in such a way that you can achieve things physically that others find more difficult.

> **Logical Smart:** You like to work by yourself; you don't really worry about other people agreeing with your beliefs; you like science, math, computers, or counting things; you like to put things in order, arrange things logically, look for patterns and relationships between things; you are good at analysis, calculation, and planning; you need things to make sense based on facts; you enjoy games like chess or checkers; you like to think about the future and what you would like to be someday.

Self Smart: You enjoy quiet time alone in thought; you understand your own motives and reasons for doing things; you like to daydream about new ideas and explore your own feelings and thoughts.

Word Smart: You love to read and tell stories or write stories or poetry; you enjoy learning other languages; you have a good vocabulary; you like to research and read about ideas that interest you; you enjoy playing word games.

Music Smart: You enjoy singing, listening to music, or playing an instrument; you remember melodies or tunes easily; you hum, whistle, or sing while doing tasks; you have good rhythm; you remember things by making up a song about them.

Picture Smart: You remember faces better than names; you like to draw, doodle, or sketch; you enjoy building things or taking things apart and putting them back together; you like working with art materials; you like watching movies, television, or video games; you enjoy looking at pictures and talking about them.

Body Smart: You like to move around and be active; you learn physical skills easily; you move while you think or talk on the phone; you enjoy acting, playing sports, and dancing gracefully; you use movement to help you remember things; you have good coordination; maybe you love recess?

People Smart: You like to watch people; you make friends easily, you offer to help others, and you enjoy group activities and conversation; you like meeting new people; you like to organize activities for you and your friends; you figure people out and what mood they are in quickly; you get concerned about issues of fairness to others; you like to help with causes that help other people.

Nature Smart: You like animals and care about nature; you like going to parks, zoos, and aquariums; you enjoy outside activities like hiking or camping and you have a good memory for where you have been and the animals, plants, and people there; you like to understand nature and your surroundings better.

Street Smart: You have a lot of common sense and know what's going on in the world. You know what every type of person has to deal with daily and you understand all groups of people and how to act around them.

Tech Smart: You like to study or are highly interested or proficient in a technical field, especially electronics, such as computers. You are able to engage with electronics with little instruction and make sense of it. You find working with computers or on the phone rewarding and fulfilling.

Financial Smart: You are interested in and even advise on financial matters. You may be good at saving money or investing. You find studying how money is transferred to be interesting. You enjoy watching the stock market, and learning about stocks, bonds, and retirement accounts.

Food Smart: You like food and like to learn about different kinds of foods and how they interact with each other. You may be considered a "foodie" and have an ardent or refined interest in food. You may seek new food experiences as a hobby rather than simply eating out of convenience or hunger. You may study food and the nutritional benefits or lack of benefits of it. You may enjoy cooking or baking.

Culture Smart: You are well-versed in and have a deep understanding of a specific culture or cultures. You know about that culture's behaviors, beliefs, and values and how they are passed from one generation to the next. You know how to interact appropriately with a specific group of people. You may enjoy learning more about your own culture or other cultures. You like attending events that are an expression or celebration of a specific culture. You may embrace diversity and celebrate other cultures.

Fashion/Beauty Smart: You like fashion and style. You like being able to alter or enhance appearances. You may study fashion magazines to learn and know about the latest trends. You may like to do hair and makeup for others. You enjoy helping choose clothes that best suit others for personal or professional needs. You like attending events or shows where models are displaying the newest styles. You have an overall or specific interest in appearances. Helping others look their best comes naturally to you and you find pleasure in it.

Communication Smart: You like to interact with others

and find it easy. You like to communicate by using different forms. You understand nuances in verbal and nonverbal communication. You may like to study written communication. You may like to speak in front of others or on camera. You can make the complicated seem clear in the way you communicate it to others. You may know more than one language. You may find the evolution of communication interesting.

Business Smart: You like learning about business. You may operate a business(es). You find articles regarding different businesses fascinating. You like learning the different facets of a business. You may like to talk about different businesses and the planning of businesses. You have great branding or marketing strategies.

Mechanical Smart: You find it easy to take things apart and put them back together. You like understanding how parts go together to make something operate. You are shown how to fix something mechanical, and you learn quickly and remember. You find it fascinating to explore how systems interact to make something run. You enjoy working on mechanical things as a career or just as a hobby.

Survival Smart: You may take an interest in learning how to live in certain situations or climates. You take precautions and prepare for trips or for the unexpected weather that may come. You have a survival kit of some sort. You are resourceful and are able to use what is around you to survive.

> **Spiritual or Religious Smart:** You have studied specific religions for personal understanding or for professional needs. You spend time practicing a religion. You have an interest in learning about different religions. You may consider yourself spiritual. Your spirituality is important to you. You spend time investigating things such as the soul, afterlife, or a supernatural being(s). Others seek guidance or understanding from you in their quest for understanding.

There are many other "smarts," and once you understand what you are good at and what excites you, you can start creating action steps to create that vision. If you are still feeling like you don't know what your purpose is or how to create a vision, it is okay. Just be willing to live alive and be open to anything and your path will present itself.

A Chinese proverb warns, "If we do not change the direction we are going, we are likely to end up where we are headed." Are you going in a direction of living your life alive? Vision and work go hand-in-hand. You can't just want something and sit back and hope for it. But you can't just do work without vision.

Create a course of action instead of a force of action. When you do so, two things tend to happen. One is that you have a dream or vision and then work for or toward it, or you commit to the work and then the vision appears. Both work. I had a vision and worked toward it. I have met others who work and then the vision appears. I met one person who worked for eighteen years before she felt nudged toward her vision. But when the time came, she was prepared with the time and resources.

Don't get caught up in the details; just trust that the vision will come. A great tip is not only to envision where you want to be, but to experience the physical sensations that go along with it. If you can envision it and feel it, you are much more likely to do what you need to do to make it happen. Don't just look at the car you want as it drives by you on the street, or stick a picture of it on a vision board. Go sit in the car you want. Heck, take it for a test drive. Drive it like it's stolen.... I mean earned! Go walk through the house you want during an open house. Go visit the city you would like to move to. Listen to music that inspires what you want. Eat food that connects you to where or what it is that you want.

When I wanted to move to Maui, first I had to decide I would. Honestly, I decided and then put the word "someday" behind it. I will move to Maui someday. Someday is not a real date, and it is nowhere to be found on a calendar. Someday is a way to pacify a deadline. If you are saying "someday," you need to check yourself. You can always move a date, but you have to set one! Once I decided I was going to move, even though I didn't believe I would be moving in 2013, I had to believe it was possible. I didn't have to believe totally; all I had to do was believe it was possible. Once I decided, I let the world know. Tell the world what you are going to do. It becomes harder to back out when you have eyes on you.

Then I decided to commit. A total commitment was what I brought to the table. When creating a vision for your life, you have to be willing to work and not just hope for it. Hope is not a success strategy. If you're not excited about your plan, it's probably not the right path. That vision should keep you awake at night and send chills up and down your spine as you share your vision with others. It has been said

LIVING YOUR LIFE ALIVE

that only a few great opportunities come along in a lifetime. We need to grab them!

Tools to make sure things happen:

1. Create specific visual reminders.
   a. Change your home screens to pictures of what you want.
   b. Change your logins or passwords to reflect what you want. But, of course, still make them difficult for others to guess.
   c. Recite affirmations daily. Recite them out loud and as if you already have what you desire.
   d. Create dream or vision boards and hang them where you will see them all of the time.
2. Read about the subject of your desire.
   a. Research! Become informed and educated about what you desire.
3. Listen to things about what you want, whether it is music or training.
4. Watch things that have to do with your vision. Watch movies, webcasts, and training videos that inspire and grow your vision.
5. Find others who have gone before you and have experienced what could benefit your effort.
6. Surround yourself with people who are for you. Limit time with people who distract you from your vision.

7. Tell others about your vision. Don't listen to naysayers; listen to people who believe in you.

Visions don't have to be a fifty-year plan. Visions can be, "The next vision I have for me is...." Actually, most of us have to practice envisioning small things and seeing them accomplished to be open to believing in bigger things. For example, let's take something simple, maybe not easy, but simple. Let's take earning a company incentive trip.

You really want this trip! This Caribbean cruise has been your dream vacation for years, and now, just by stretching a bit, you could earn it. Right when you think of the idea, a negative thought or thoughts are likely to pop up and cause you to give up. Identify them and trash them. Once you have trashed the negative ideas, do the following:

1. Change your computer screen and phone screen to pictures of the ship. Set a daily reminder on your phone to remind you by having it say out loud, "It is October 1st, and I am now boarding the ship that is going to take me on my dream vacation."

2. Change passwords to Cruise+Year. For example, Cruise2016

3. Listen to Caribbean music while imagining dancing on the cruise deck by the pool.

4. Watch videos from the cruise website. Take virtual tours and imagine yourself there and enjoying it. Search sites such as YouTube to find videos that others have posted. Plan excursions and events on the ship.

5. Read reviews. Find others who have earned a trip. This will remind you that it is possible. Ask them for tips to help you earn the trip.

6. Tell your family and friends you are earning a trip. Listen to others who are there for you and ask them to hold you accountable.

7. And finally, go for it!

Remember, work and vision go hand-in-hand. You can't just envision it; you have to work at it.

What is the worst thing that could happen if you put these tools into practice and you missed the target? Even if you missed, you would be further along than where you were.

You can apply these tools to anything! What do you want? Play with these tools. They work! I know you will be amazed by what happens. They are easy to do. They are also easy not to do.

Sometimes creating a vision can seem overwhelming. Sometimes we have no idea where to start. Is it possible to open yourself to all possibilities? No limits. Just be open to accepting what comes. Your vision or visions are yours. No one can take that away.

Whenever I feel the nudge and know I need to create a vision and plan, I become overwhelmed immediately. The emergency brake comes on. There is a scripture I often recall that reminds me it will all be okay.

"For I know the plans I have for you," declares the LORD,
"PLANS TO PROSPER YOU AND NOT TO HARM YOU,
PLANS TO GIVE YOU HOPE AND A FUTURE."

— Jeremiah 29:11

Find something inspiring you can read and memorize to recall when the emergency brake comes on to tell you to go for it.

Don't try to be like anyone else. Everyone else is taken. Discover you! The world is waiting.

"Only the truth of who you are, if realized, will set you free."

— Eckhart Tolle

Exercise:

Who is it you look up to?

_____

_____

_____

_____

What is it you look forward to?

_____

_____

_____

_____

_____

What does chasing yourself ten years from now look like?

_____
_____
_____
_____
_____
_____
_____
_____
_____

What smart(s) are you?

_____
_____
_____
_____
_____
_____

Name one way you could choose to practice visualization tools.

_____
_____
_____
_____
_____
_____
_____
_____

When is the exact time you are going to implement these tools?

_____
_____
_____
_____
_____
_____
_____
_____
_____
_____

List the tools you are going to implement:

_____
_____
_____
_____
_____
_____
_____
_____
_____

CHAPTER SIXTEEN

TAKING ALL KINDS OF STEPS

"When it is obvious that the goals cannot be reached,
don't adjust the goals; adjust the action steps."

— Confucius

Steps forward, steps to the side, steps backward are all steps. Your first step, baby steps, sustainable steps, stair steps, and dance steps are all steps we learn. Steps through success, love, grief, parenting, and education are all steps we may experience at some time in our lives.

I used to believe that steps forward are the only steps that matter or make a difference. I had one speed and it was forward. What steps are you comfortable taking? Are you walking backwards? Every step we take in life, whether big or small, forward or backward, makes a difference. Sometimes, we even take a step of pause. We are on this journey to learn, and each step teaches us something important. Embrace each step.

The steps I want to talk to you about are the steps to becoming the best you. We are usually taking steps toward or away from being the best we can be. Moving in the direction you are called to take is simply a decision. Once the decision is made and you are ready to accept the abundance that is waiting for you, you can start taking the steps that will take you there. The key is to count the steps. Not just the steps that move you forward. All steps move you forward if you choose. You are only allowed to count the steps. Steps equal activity. Activity makes a difference.

One of the first quotes I read when I started my business, and I live by it daily, was Eleanor Roosevelt's advice to: "Do one thing every day that scares you." It doesn't really matter how big or small or in what area you practice this action. It is just about learning what you are made of. One day, I did a really big hill climb on a snowmobile. It scared me, but I did it anyway. I didn't care about making it to the top of the mountain or becoming better at snowmobiling. I did it because I promised myself I would do one thing that scared me every day. Even though climbing hills on a snowmobile doesn't seem to have anything to do with my business, it really had everything to do with building my business. I am often scared of picking up the phone and calling a potential client, but I do it anyway. Do you know why? Because I first committed to the action and I saw clearly what was on the other side of that action. At times, we fall into doing what only feels good or comfortable. That leads to a life of mediocrity.

Zig Ziglar says, "If you aim at nothing, you will hit it every time." We need to be clear on what we are aiming for with our goals. We don't get to walk up to our buffet of fears and pick a few morsels, then expect results. We need to take it all in. Experiencing each fear makes us grow. You can't stay the person you are today and get where you want go. You need to stretch. Feeling the fear and doing whatever scares you anyway is liberating. We are the boss, the author, and the puppeteer of ourselves. We might as well feel great about ourselves. In her book Choices, Nancy Bryne says, "You don't have to move mountains, you don't have to save the world. Your job is to have the best life you can possibly have, and everything else will follow."

Here are the steps for achieving whatever you set out to pursue:

1. Decide.

2. Commit.

3. Create and ask for a clear vision.

4. Visualize daily what your goal will look like, smell like, sound like, and feel like.

5. Ask for and accept help. Find people who have gone before you in a certain area and ask them for help. Speaker and author Rita Davenport used to tell me, "Don't take advice from someone more messed up than you." We need to reach out and above to get sound advice.

6. Create a passion for improvement and invest in yourself. Become a PRO! If you are seeking financial success, become a pro. If you have health goals you are not meeting, become a pro. If you want to live a life of total time freedom, become a pro. Improve daily. Learning is improving even if it doesn't appear you are moving forward.

7. Feel the fear and do it anyway!

When your courage is not bigger than your fear, then your faith has to be! Sometimes the smallest step in the right direction ends up being the biggest step of your life. Tiptoe if you must, but take the step. Taking these steps will allow you to step into those amazing shoes right in front of you. They may look too big for you now, but they are not.

P – Push
U – Until
S – Something
H – Happens

Beware the Dream Stealers

I must warn you, if you haven't experienced it already, there are dream stealers lurking everywhere. They seem to pop up right when you get ready to take a step in the direction of your dreams. When you make the decision and you tell people, or they see what you are doing, they all of a sudden have a lot to say about what you are about to do. I would say that most of these dream stealers don't really mean you any harm, but if you listen to them, it can cause a lot of harm. Many times, these people are close to you and may even have your best interest at heart. However, they aren't in your shoes. They are probably not paying your bills or have never attempted to do what you want to do. In many cases, people don't want you leaving the comfort zone that all of you are in together because it makes them look at their own lives and causes them discomfort. You may hear things like: "That is too risky." "You don't actually think you can make money doing one of those things?" "You have just experienced a huge loss; are you sure now is the right time?" "You are willing to give up your cushy job with benefits to go out on your own?" "You have never done anything like this before, so what makes you think you can succeed?" "You are totally under-qualified to go for that position!" "What will others think?" and "I don't think, at your age, this is a smart move."

Some of what others say may offend you. Don't catch and hang on to the offense. It can bury you. Just let the offense bounce off of you while you give the dream stealers a good show. They may be trying to steal your dreams, but you might just be inspiring them to live out their dreams. Remember, you were called to walk out your dreams! If I listened to the dream stealers, not only would my life look a lot different, but many other lives would look very different as well.

I'm not just suggesting you try your dreams out. I am begging you to walk them out. I actually believe it is your responsibility. One of my favorite sayings is: "Don't let the noise of others' opinions drown out your own inner voice. And most important, have the courage to follow your heart and intuition." Lions don't lose sleep over the opinions of sheep, so why should you?

Exercise:

What decision do you need to make to move forward? Or in what area is there a decision that needs to be made?

_____
_____
_____
_____

Are you willing to commit to making that decision happen? What specifically does that commitment look like?

_____
_____
_____
_____
_____
_____
_____

Have you created and experienced a vision for your life? If so, write the summary here. If not, when specifically are you going to take the time to create it?

_____
_____
_____
_____
_____
_____
_____

Who do you need to make this happen? Who do you need to ask for help or bring along to make it work?

_____
_____
_____
_____
_____
_____
_____

What fear do you feel when thinking about moving forward with your vision?

_____

_____

_____

_____

_____

_____

_____

_____

Who are the current dream stealers in your life? Who would surface and cast doubt if you started living life outside of your comfort zone?

_____

_____

_____

_____

_____

_____

_____

_____

CHAPTER SEVENTEEN

HEALTHY LIVING

"Number one, like yourself. Number two, you have to eat healthy.
And number three, you've got to squeeze your buns.
That's my formula."

— Richard Simmons

Are you healthy? Are you happy with your appearance? Do you look into the mirror and think about all the things you wish could be different? What are the things you would like to change? What are you willing to do to make those changes? If it doesn't challenge you, it won't change you.

"The only people who like change are babies with dirty diapers."

— Rita Davenport

Before we dive into discussing true healthy living, I would like us to start from a place of gratitude and appreciation. Although it is easy to focus on things we don't like or areas we would change or could improve, it is just as important to appreciate our magnificent bodies. Just think about how we have 37 trillion cells, take over 20,000 breaths a day, and our heart beats just for us…103,680 beats in twenty-four hours. Just think what your eyes are seeing today. Were you able to hear the voice of your loved ones? Just look at what your fingers have already done for you today. They are flipping these pages for you. Your ten toes have taken you to some great places in your life. Take this moment and just thank your body for everything it has done for you already today.

Wow! It is truly amazing. Your body hears everything your mind says. How can we live our life alive and feel great about ourselves when all we do is beat ourselves up? Give yourself a break and be thankful! Close your eyes, take a deep breath, open your eyes, look at your body, and say out loud, "Thank you." That's not so hard. Be kind to your body. It's the only one you have!

You are individually and wonderfully made, so quit comparing yourself to others!

Mark Sterling says, "If you want to soar in life, you must first learn to F.L.Y. First Love Yourself." This is the same concept as putting on your air mask first during an emergency on an airplane. We must first take care of ourselves before we can help others.

Your body also loves healthy living. How do we know what that truly means? We are inundated with information on food, exercise, and supplements. Where do we start? We start by making a decision. It can just be a decision about a lifestyle, not a fad or a diet. Whatever the decision is, fitness guru Jane Fonda says, "It's never too late—never too late to start over, never too late to be happy." Let's put things in perspective. You can recreate almost any part of your body to be like brand new. Certain cells in your body actually die and new ones are created. Recent studies have shown that few cells live as long as the individual they belong to without renewal. A majority, if not all, of the cells making up the cerebral cortex belong to this small group. The lifespans of some other human cells are as follows:

- Stomach lining cells — 2 days
- Sperm cells — 2-3 days
- Colon cells — 3-4 days
- Skin epidermal cells — 2-4 weeks
- Lymphocytes — 2 months to a year
- Red blood cells — 4 months
- Pancreas cells — 1 year or more
- Bone Cells — 25-30 years

Are you open to living and feeling a different way or are you holding on to a certain identity about your body? Perhaps you are holding on to your appearance, your weight, your illness, or a certain identity. Maybe it is holding you back from living alive.

"When I let go of who I am,
I become what I might be."

— Lao Tzu

We can't talk about living healthy and not talk about food. Here is a simple way to explain in simple terms how our body processes food. Our bodies separate all foods and their contents into one of two categories: nutrient or toxin. Obviously, nutrients are preferred so choose carefully. Toxins are anything that can't be used as energy in the body. The food we eat is fuel or poison. One thing we can do to help us feel our best so we can live our best is to choose to eat clean.

To understand what clean eating looks like, we need to understand the difference between whole foods vs. man food. In summary:

> **Man Food:** Man's food is processed. It's food-like products. It's really "fake" food manufactured in a plant to resemble "real" food. Man's food is also real food that has been altered with chemicals or sprayed with pesticides. Our bodies do not know how to process much of this food.

> **Good Food (God Food):** This food is natural and not created by humans. It is organic or free-range and has no added hormones or antibiotics. They are simply foods that have not been altered.

Ann Wigmore, holistic health practitioner and nutritionist, warns, "The food you eat can be either the safest and most powerful form of medicine or the slowest form of poison."

We get attached to our bodies as part of our identity, but really our bodies don't even exist over time. Isn't that awesome? It is weird to think that our five-year-old body, twenty-year-old body, or thirty-year-old body is not even there anymore! We can create a new us, so we can't make excuses and say, "This is just the way I am."

It is so easy to live an unhealthy lifestyle, but it can become just as easy to live a healthy one. First of all, you have to know you are worth it. Do you know you are worth it?

Find out what makes you "tick" when it comes to healthy living. Instead of making it a chore, find out what you like doing. What do you eat that makes your body feels its best? Where are you? Where do you like to shop for your food? How do mega stores, grocery stores, or farmers' markets make you feel? Where do you eat when you are truly enjoying eating? Are you eating what you truly know benefits your body, or have you given in to others' eating habits just because you live or work with them? Do you choose things you think you should eat, or do you stop and ask your body what it would like? Do you rest when your body needs rest, or do you decide it doesn't need rest and push on? Do you move when your body needs to move, or do you make excuses and allow other things to get in the way? What if you gave your body the movement it desired? What, physically, do you enjoy doing? Do you like crushing it at the gym or taking dance lessons? Do you like exercising with others or working out in your home? Exercise can be seen as a treat and not a chore. What physical activity have you done where you catch yourself smiling while doing it? Do more of it! There are so many activities to choose from, so pick ones that make you happy, and stay close to anything that makes you glad you are alive.

When you travel for work or pleasure, how does your body feel? Do you give it what it needs? Do you prepare before, during, and after travel to stay on track? Do you listen and remember what your body needed last time you traveled? Maybe it was an extra day on each side of the trip to adjust to the surroundings and decompress.

What do you do to feel grounded? Do you take deep breaths? Pray or meditate? Spend time alone? Sit or lay on the ground? When we are grounded, we can see better results.

We all have different "engine speeds." Recognize when your engine is running at its best so you can work and create during this time. Recognize when your engine needs rest to hit the reset button. Also, recognize other people around you and their engine speeds. Does being around a certain person stimulate your energy levels or suck your tank dry? Take a moment to recognize the speed of your engine right now and just be thankful for the place you are right now. Take a moment to recognize any changes you need to make to protect your engine speed. Are you at your optimal speed? Your engine speed is part of you. Be true to it and protect it. Don't slow down because everyone around you is going slower, and don't feel pressure to speed up because people seem to be passing you. Be true to your engine.

How much do you sleep? Is that amount serving you? Are you sleeping too much, and do you lack motivation? Are you waking at night with unsettled thoughts? Create a vision for your life that serves you and serves others, so you jump out of bed in the morning rested and ready to take on the day!

Nutrition, exercise, and sleep are the basics. Many times we search for things that will make us feel better or make us happy, but we skip the basics. These basics are pretty important for the foundation of your day and because days turn into weeks, months, and years, it is worth checking yourself and caring for yourself in these areas. If you need assistance in these areas, feel free to seek assistance from people who can provide tools to help. A session with a coach or trainer, a specific product, or a program can provide you the basics you desire. Just take a moment to reflect and implement the basics.

Put "me" time on the calendar. Do you know what to do during "me" time? Running errands to cross things off your "to do" lists doesn't count. Getting your nails done or spending time in the man cave may count a little bit, but what are the things that really fill you up? What are the things that help you hit the refresh button? What would it take for you to become a priority in your life?

We don't live in our bodies. We are bigger than our bodies, but our bodies are precious things that allow us to do what we need to do.

Eat like you love yourself. Move like you love yourself. Speak like you love yourself. Act like you love yourself. Love like you love yourself. Succeed like you love yourself. Live Alive like you love yourself!

Exercise:

Name three things about your body you're most thankful for:

1. _____

2. _____

3. _____

Name three things about your appearance you love:

1. _____

2. _____

3. _____

Name places where you enjoy shopping for food and why:

_____
_____
_____
_____
_____
_____
_____
_____

Name physical activities you enjoy and why you enjoy them:

_____
_____
_____
_____
_____
_____
_____
_____
_____
_____
_____

Is there anything from "the basics" (nutrition, exercise, and sleep) that you need to pause and take care of so you can live your life fully alive?

_____

_____

_____

_____

_____

_____

_____

_____

_____

_____

_____

_____

_____

_____

_____

_____

_____

CHAPTER EIGHTEEN

LEADING IS A CHOICE

"I've always considered myself to be just average talent and what I have is a ridiculous insane obsessiveness for practice and preparation."

— Will Smith

Where do leaders come from?

Great leadership is about choosing to do the work. You don't have to possess a certain title, rank, position, or class to be a great leader. Plenty of people possess certain titles who are not great leaders. You just have to be willing to get your hands dirty and do the work. You have to be willing to do things others aren't willing to do. Don't let what you cannot do keep you from doing what you can. What are you truly made of?

Leaders don't just fall on the top of the mountain; they have to climb there. It is all part of the journey. Let's explore the mountain. Let's even explore doing something fun on the mountain once we climb it. Let's fly down the mountain on a pair of skis or a snowboard. Can you envision being at the top of the mountain and being able to see peak after peak covered in pure white snow as the sun sparkles through snowflakes drifting slowly through the sky? It is a winter wonderland! Can you feel the crisp air in your lungs as you take a deep breath? Can you believe you are at the top looking down 10,000 feet? It is truly breathtaking.

If the journey started with a different narrative, it would provide a very different, but much more realistic picture. Can you imagine shopping the day before to get all of your cold weather gear? Can you imagine getting up at 4:00 a.m. to get ahead of traffic for the two-hour drive to the base of the mountain? Can you believe how much lift tickets cost? Can you believe these lift lines already? It is freezing cold and you can barely feel your fingertips. As you climb the mountain, the view starts to appear, and it is truly breathtaking. As you get off the lift, you decide it has been worth it. You start down the mountain and feel the rush of flying down a mountain on skis or a board. It is so much fun until you catch an edge and you are sliding down the mountain on your behind instead of your feet. You get down, and you try it again. You climb all the way up, and you ski or board down. When you get to the top again, you remember to pause and look around at God's masterpiece. It is truly breathtaking from the top. You go down, and this time you can't feel your body because your muscles are spent. You have to drive home, unpack, clean up, and you still have a few hours of work to do before you can go to bed, but that breathtaking view made it all worthwhile.

You ended up at the top again because you did the work to get there. You get to experience the whole mountain. You made the decision and made it happen.

Leaders can't just be at the top or tell everyone how to get to the top; they have to do the work and show others how to get there. Everyone would like to experience the top of some mountain, or some wonderful place he or she dreams of, but the work stops most people. This is where we find out what we are made of. You go to the top because of the work you are willing to do. You most likely will never feel like preparing, but you do it anyway.

Few people feel adequate to lead, and if they do, they probably think they have arrived. An Afghan proverb says, "If you think you're leading and no one is following you, then you're only taking a walk." Leadership is a journey, not a destination. When you feel inadequate and accept help, you can move along with your journey in leadership. You must first be a great leader to yourself before you can be a great leader to others.

One way you can tell whether you are comfortable being you and accepting where you are in the leadership journey is when you are in a group of people who are "more advanced" than you, and it makes you feel inspired instead of inadequate. It is when you feel proud of what you have overcome, instead of ashamed of where you are, that you begin to embody true leadership qualities.

Why is leadership important? Leading is the ability to influence and inspire others. You have the opportunity and honor of leading from right where you are. You can make a difference in others' lives right now if you wish. Identify others who are open to learning more and being more. Identify others who are hungry for living their lives alive.

We cannot motivate people, period. We may sprinkle some motivation on people, but it usually lasts about as long as it takes to shower—not long. There are three reasons motivation doesn't last:

1. You try something and experience negative results.

2. You are excited about something, but get distracted by something and lose the excitement.

3. You try but "it's hard," so you end up justifying why you need to settle for less.

Motivation won't last, but we can make the decision to do what we set out to do and inspire people by what we demonstrate.

Regardless of where you are in life, you've had bad days or bad things happen to you. We've all thrown ourselves "pity parties." I will give you a few moments, okay maybe a few hours, to wallow in your pity pad. However, do not set up camp or furnish this place. Please don't invite others in. These are not places you want to dwell; these are places of reflection and attitude adjustment. It does not serve you in any way to stick around. I am sorry for what you went through, or what you are going through, or even what you may go through, but life is not about what happens to us; life is about how we respond to each event. Finding your way out inspires others. Leaders see the silver lining in a situation and use the situation to grow. Showing others what you have overcome inspires them.

Exercise:

Do you consider yourself a leader?

_____
_____
_____
_____
_____
_____
_____
_____

Where is your circle of influence?

_____
_____
_____
_____
_____
_____
_____

Are you doing the work necessary to have an effect on others?

_____
_____
_____
_____
_____
_____
_____

TAKING A LEAP OF FAITH

"Twenty years from now you will be more disappointed by the things you didn't do than by the ones you did do. So throw off the bowlines. Sail away from the safe harbor. Catch the trade winds in your sails. Explore. Dream. Discover."

— Mark Twain

"Faith is the assurance of things hoped for, and the conviction of things not seen."

— Hebrews 11:1

Imagine being in a car and driving on a long, winding road. You can see in front of you, but only as far as the next bend. You can see behind you, but only as far as the last curve. What if you looked in the rearview mirror more than the windshield? That sounds silly, but many of us do it. Don't look backwards; you aren't going that way! It is there for a quick glimpse of where you came from. It is what you have overcome and a place you can reflect on quickly, so you can be thankful for the lessons you learned in that part of your journey. Keep your eyes on the road and trust that even though you can't see the entire road in front of you, you can have faith that the journey is worth taking.

There are times when looking in the rearview mirror might be needed. Please pull over to do this. We need to know when to stop for a pit stop along the road. If we keep experiencing the same troubles, we need to figure out why. What haven't you let go of that is holding your trip back?

Hindsight is not always 20/20 if you aren't learning the lessons. Hindsight is learning, and then it becomes 20/20. What patterns do you keep repeating that you need to figure out? Behavioral patterns and choices will keep repeating if you don't catch the lesson. Stop, catch the lesson, and move forward. Lessons are fun to gather up. What if we could look at lessons as a treasure hunt and not like, "You had better learn your lesson," from an upset parent. Then, when looking back doesn't interest you anymore, you're doing something right and you can move along on your journey.

Do you feel this thing holding you back? It could feel like trying to move forward with a rubber band attached to your belt pulling you back. Is it forgiveness? Forgiveness is never about letting someone else off the hook; it is about letting you off the hook. It may be hard for you to forgive or show grace toward someone who hurt you or let you down. Are you on the hook? You deserve to be free. It is not fair that someone else offended you, lied to you, betrayed you, took advantage of you, stole from you, or abandoned you. However, it is even worse if you stay on the hook. You deserve to be free. Is the offense more important than your life? Is it robbing you of your life? Could I ask you to lay it down? Lay it down and live your best life! I know it's not fair, but you are worth it. Karma will take care of the rest. I'm sure you've heard people say that karma is a bitch, but it isn't if you are on the right side of it! Trust it.

I also recommend taking a quick look back when you are stuck in past experiences or stories. Maybe you failed in the past and you are projecting that failure into the future. Or are you living in past successes? Are you riding what you succeeded at years ago and not creating new wins? Maybe you think you are past your prime and have done all you can do, but are you just going to ride that wave? Maybe you believe you are just a "has been" and you've been put out to pasture. The past is the past. Look through the windshield and see where you are going. What is in front of you?

Looking ahead will give you a much better view. Every positive change in your life begins with a clear decision that you are either going to do something or stop doing something.

Find others who may have taken a similar road to help guide you. But, above all, trust God. If God started good work in you, God will give you the resources to complete it.

Margaret Shepard, an author, artist, and calligrapher, once said, "Sometimes your only available transportation is a leap of faith." This is so true! However, there is a difference between bravery and recklessness. You have to be honest about where you are in life and make good choices. It would be great if we all had an accurate crystal ball, but we don't, so all we can do is take ownership of our decisions.

Build that safety net of accountability by telling people what you are planning on accomplishing and when.

There will always be something there to distract you. Even good things can be a distraction. Being dialed in is so important to accomplishing what you want. We have to have faith and focus to get where we need to go.

What would it take for you to live like you were a dog who realized someone left the gate open? Where would you go? What would you do? The whole world is yours.

Yume Tran, a good friend and entrepreneur, took a leap in her life. At the age of fourteen, she was sent out of Vietnam and spent thirteen months in various refugee camps in Indonesia before a great foster family sponsored her to move to the United States. Her siblings and parents escaped the same way shortly after. Without money or much fluency in English, her family started a lawn care business. Yume, her sisters, and brother worked hard to help their parents while going to college. It taught her the importance of a good work ethic. She graduated and went to work for a major systems integration and consulting company. Although she climbed the corporate ladder in America, she started feeling unsettled. She kept feeling the nudge to do more. She met with a life coach who asked her, "What do you like to do? What are you good at?" Yume replied, "I would like to do something on my own, utilizing the skills and experience the corporate world has given me."

Yume will tell you that opening a restaurant was not a brilliant idea, given she does not like to cook and restaurants don't pay much right

CHAPTER 19 - TAKING A LEAP OF FAITH

out of the gate. But she jumped in with both feet, learning how to cook in a commercial kitchen along the way. Although she definitely was not prepared, she and her husband were willing to work very hard, refusing to fail. Their hard work, perseverance, and focus paid off. They now have a restaurant with a loyal following and a new, smaller one offering roll-your-own sushi. Yume did all this while completing her cookbook, doing a cooking show on the local Fox channel, and manufacturing a line of fifteen Asian sauces. Yume will tell you she found the passion for the restaurant business after all these years of dreaming and working toward the dream of having her own business and making people happy. She took the leap of faith, worked hard, and is now living her life alive.

Speak life into your life! Speak life into your vision!

I have been scared every time I've decided to leap. Every leap has been way out of my comfort zone. Whether it was being a victim advocate, or making the decision to start my own business, I had to make a decision and commit. I was doing my best at juggling my job, business, and family. My business was building momentum, so I started to see the difference the business was making for my family and other families I was working with. I knew in order to take my business to the next level, I needed to go all in. Once I made the decision, I had to tell others. I had to tell my family I was leaving a career I had worked hard to be in and the security of a job with benefits. I also knew I had to give up my volunteer position. At the time, I was serving on the board of Hope House of Colorado. We were getting ready to break ground on a house where teen moms could stay with their children for a year and receive support. I had to give up something good I was doing to go create something great.

I took the leap, even though it was kind of messy. Most of them are. But the rush you experience when you leap is like no other rush you will ever experience. You feel the excitement of hope and then start experiencing amazing things that unfold because you leaped.

"Leap and the net will appear."

— Zen Saying

Exercise:

Can you identify any places in your life where you are looking through the rearview mirror?

_____
_____
_____
_____
_____
_____
_____
_____
_____
_____
_____
_____
_____
_____
_____
_____
_____
_____
_____

Is there anything distracting you from being focused on where you need to be focused? Is that distraction or distractions something you can change?

_____

_____

_____

_____

_____

_____

_____

_____

_____

Is there something you need to give up to go up?

_____

_____

_____

_____

_____

_____

_____

_____

CHAPTER TWENTY

COMING FULL CIRCLE

*"Don't judge each day by the harvest
you reap but by the seeds that you plant."*

— Robert Louis Stevenson

I f I know one thing about the show of life, it is to trust. I know—easier said than done. However, if we trust, then not only should we sit back and enjoy the show, but we should grab a bucket of popcorn! Whenever I have hoped, wished, envisioned, prayed, and most importantly...when I have trusted and let go of the control... things have turned out better than I could imagine. Sooner or later, we will get what we expect, so expect to live your life alive.

Coming full circle is really just about being able to connect the dots. How much fun can we have seeing how things line up to assist us on our journey when we trust? All of your worry is for nothing. New Zealand cricket great Glenn Turner says, "Worrying is like a rocking chair, it gives you something to do, but gets you nowhere." In short, worrying doesn't allow you to live life alive.

When I was a child, I loved dot-to-dot games. It was so much fun starting at the beginning and watching as the dots were connected and the image appeared. Sometimes, I even started at the end and counted backwards, but either way, all of the dots had to be connected in order for the picture to appear as intended. This is the fun of living your life alive. You can connect the dots and have fun doing it. Each dot is an experience. Some dots may not feel as great as others, but you get to experience every dot. How much fun could you have experiencing life as a fun treasure hunt of collecting experiences along the way?

If you are on the right side of karma, ride the wave. If not, then find grace and accept it. You are worth it. Regardless of how bad the choice or action you made, you are worth what is on the other side of it. Your past does not equal your future.

Your best days are yet to come!

I hope this book has served to help you explore, identify, and inspire you to live your life alive. And know that you are not alone in the process of living your life alive. But the truth is, as Glinda the Good Witch says in *The Wizard of Oz*, "You've always had the power...."

CHAPTER TWENTY-ONE
INTERVIEWS WITH PEOPLE LIVING LIFE ALIVE

"Surround yourself with the dreamers and the doers, the believers and thinkers, but most of all, surround yourself with those who see the greatness within you, even when you don't see it yourself."

— Edmund Lee

Before we end our journey together, I want to share with you some of the fascinating people I have met who embody the idea of "living your life alive." I was privileged to interview these people, some in person, some via email, and I have included the full transcripts of their interviews or simply summarized and quoted the high points. I hope you will find them inspiring examples to draw strength and courage from in your own quest to live your life alive.

Kimokeo Kapahulehua — Hawaiian Culturist

I was honored to "talk story" with Kimokeo and now share that conversation with you. Kimokeo is one of the most influential Hawaiians living today—and he is not only living, but also living his life alive and helping others do the same.

Kimokeo's influence stretches globally. He has a passion for extending the life of the land and the ocean. He teaches in many ways, but always with a hands-on approach. He spends some of his days in an outrigger canoe, teaching others how to paddle the open waters. He works diligently to conserve the fishponds on Maui. There are many days you can find him volunteering or working in the community teaching Hawaiian culture.

When speaking about what allows people to live their lives alive and what holds others back, Kimokeo has some great wisdom to share. He believes our culture has an effect on the world and we need to choose to interact with our culture. There is the "economic culture" and an "inner culture" (inner-self). People who tend to spend a lot of time in the economic culture can experience a lot of conflict with self and others. People who spend time within the inner culture have a better sense of self and what makes them truly happy.

If we allow ourselves to focus on our inner self, we can stay in a much more loving state. As humans, we should be able to have loving conversations with each other, and that is enough. Speaking and interacting with each other should feel like going to the gas station and getting filled up. These simple things are easily overlooked in an economic culture. He has also concluded that none of us really wants conflict or confrontation, but when we engage in this manner, we burn energy and, therefore, lose the ability to live life alive.

In speaking with me about entrepreneurship, Kimokeo continued to have insight and offered questions to ask ourselves. I invite you to ponder some of these ideas and ask yourself some of these questions.

Kimokeo offered that we all possess the same amount of time and have a certain amount of energy inside each of us. So whether we work for someone else or ourselves, we need to focus on loving the work we do. Kimokeo has worked for others at times as well as for himself. "You get to live that day, so are you doing what you love?" We have the opportunity to express ourselves through our work. Are you expressing yourself through your work, or are others guiding your expression? Working for someone else may give you a set schedule, defined duties, and some financial security, while working for yourself, in an unknown position, may be fearful. But the first thing you need to ask yourself is, "Am I larger than my current position?"

Your breath ("Ha" in Hawaiian) is your own. It is your breath, so no one else can own it. You shouldn't be afraid to use your own breath. Quality of life is yours for the taking. Why would you work harder for someone else than you would for yourself? Why would you give someone else more energy than you would give yourself? You will also be able to reach more people. You might be sharing your gifts with the people you work with, but how many more people could you reach? As Kimokeo says, "When I worked for others, I made a difference, but now I have expanded my impact."

When I asked Kimokeo about fear, he gave a beautiful, yet simple answer. He said he connects with people who are afraid of the ocean all of the time. Yet, there is only land and the ocean on Earth. If someone doesn't overcome the fear of the ocean, he is only half the person because he only experiences half of what is offered. A person becomes a whole person by overcoming his or her fear. We all have fear at different times.

For example, if a gun were pointed at your face, you would most likely experience fear, but the fear we are talking about is the fear that is inside of you, holding you back. To overcome this fear, you must look at it as experiencing the ocean. You can practice and take small steps. What you have to do first is find your *mana* (power within) on land and where you feel comfortable. Identify that strength and know that you can take it with you wherever you go. You can now go in the ocean when the water is calm and only go in a few feet deep. It is better than never going in because you can experience the essence of the ocean, even if it is just a little. You have to practice. You are using the *mana* in the half of yourself and just need to practice transferring the *mana* to the other side of yourself. The ocean and land do not discriminate who should experience the wholeness of them. We need both. We all can find our *mana* and experience the whole self. We can all overcome. We need to give ourselves the opportunity to grow. Kimokeo concludes by saying, "No discussion of this will really help; only facing and experiencing your fear will change you." The ocean is a place of space. You can be a free bird there. No one is there telling you what direction you can and can't go. It is a place you can be free. So why not you? Why would you only experience where you feel safe?

He continued to share a story of a canoe trip that he took off the beautiful coast of Kauai. As the sun was setting and the darkness was coming, so was a squall. Many of the paddlers expressed concern and even fear. He told them that, yes, indeed, the squall was coming, but to focus on what comes right after, which is always a nice flat ocean. And that is what happened. They stayed, experienced the squall, and saw that they could be surprised by facing their own fear and overcoming it. They found out they were more courageous than they knew.

As Kimokeo sat back and relaxed into the next story, his delight was obvious through his expressions. He told me many people ask him how it is he can go out and just paddle a canoe for hours and hours without tiring and stay so calm with so many of the unknown things out on the open sea. He answered by saying, "Because they went before us." Although we might not know our ancestors, they are with us. He just thinks about what his great-grandfather must have done with his mind or hands with the resources he had. He knows that many of his ancestors were doing what he is doing, years and years ago. He draws on their strength because it is now in him. He encourages you to draw on the strengths of those who have gone before you.

Kimokeo has a passion for paddling and for teaching others from around the world. He said he is passionate about teaching others because when he was young, he couldn't compete as a *keiki* (child). Today, *na keiki* (children) have many more opportunities to do what they would like, but not all *na keiki*. Many *na keiki* still don't have the opportunity to learn how to navigate the ocean or land. The minds of children are amazing, and we all need to help them discover what they like and what their strengths are so they can share them with the world whenever they want and not be restricted by their ages, resources, or opportunities. They shouldn't have to wait to be their true selves. Kimokeo knew then that he had much to offer in a canoe and beyond, and today, he doesn't want anyone held back from being able to do what he or she loves.

When asked directly "What does living your life alive mean?", Kimokeo responded, "Aloha. Aloha is love, respect, care, and share. Living your life alive means Aloha with passion. It is not just for Hawaiians, but a way of life that anybody can live by."

To learn more about Kimokeo, visit: http://familyofthewaa.com

Rita Davenport — Author, Speaker, Award-Winning Humorist, and Entrepreneur

Rita Davenport resides in Arizona and travels internationally as a speaker. She is a charter member of the National Speakers Association, with the distinct recognition of CSP and CPAE, and is considered to be in the top 1 percent of all paid professional speakers. She is listed in the National Speakers Association Hall of Fame.

Davenport has written four bestselling books with sales of over one million copies, including *Making Time, Making Money,* and her newest book, *Funny Side Up*, published by *Success* magazine.

Shields: What was it that "nudged" you to become an entrepreneur?

Davenport: When I was very young I felt something inside of me that I knew I had to share with others. I even set a goal to "impact the world!" I wasn't clear on what it was I would eventually do with my life, and I really didn't feel like I had a lot of talent in any specific area, but I still just knew something was there. I definitely didn't know it was entrepreneurship! That was a rewarding wakeup call! Many people around me when I was younger did things that would have normally caused discouragement, but I just knew I was meant for more. Though I was always ambitious.... In high school, I had a counselor tell me I wasn't all that smart academically and for me not to plan to go college. Raised in poverty, I even had a family member tell me not to try to get above my "raisin'," and not to get my "hopes up" about ever making something out of myself. I always wondered, "What good are low hopes?" LOL. Still, I just couldn't shake the calling on my life. I always knew we are sent into this world with a purpose and all the necessary skills and talent to fulfill that purpose. I always felt that folks who don't feel good about themselves aren't using their talents to fulfill their purposes.

I managed to graduate from college with honors and received a B.S. degree, which really came in handy, since I went on to become a motivational speaker—after being a teacher, social worker, broadcaster, and author.

After speaking for several hundred direct sales companies, though, I realized that my gift as a public speaker, broadcaster, and author wasn't necessarily duplicable, but the opportunity for anyone to succeed was available to all in direct sales. I realized it was a level playing field for anyone with enough desire. The "how to succeed" in this industry is possible when individuals are clear about their "why," and if they have enough personal desire, they will be inspired, motivated, and captivated. I was sold! This was my remedy for survivor's guilt, since I'd already achieved a measure of success by then, but had family and friends who were still struggling.

Shields: What wasn't working for you in your life that was holding you back from being the best you?

Davenport: I knew being poor wasn't working for me. How was I supposed to help others if I couldn't even feed myself? I wanted to give, and I knew if it was meant to be, it was up to me! I had a burning desire to have more, be more, learn more, do more, and earn more so I could share more. I felt such gratitude to God for his many blessings and wanted to figure out a way to give back!

Shields: What are some of your best success tips?

Davenport: First, be true to yourself. Don't listen to the naysayers. They aren't paying your bills anyway. You have a unique calling on your life. God doesn't make junk.

Secondly, hang around with successful people. (If that's not possible, listen to CDs and read biographies of successful people.) That's what I did. I listened to Earl Nightingale's *Lead the Field* tape program over and over. Now, ask yourself, "Who are the five closest people that you surround yourself with?" Always remember one pessimist can pull ten optimists down easier than one optimist can pull one pessimist up! I have had the opportunity to meet some of the most famous people in the world. People's titles or class never impressed me or bothered me, but the way people lived their lives and their ability to impact the world in a positive way were the things I watched and followed. Those are the people I wanted to be around. The world is a hard enough place, so try to surround yourself with positive people. When someone says something negative to you, say to yourself, "Cancel!" Then see the situation in your mind's eye the way you choose it to be. Don't turn your power over to others to determine how you feel about yourself. I also advise, "Don't take advice from someone more messed up than you!"

Thirdly, what you think about you bring about. Mind your mind! Energy follows thoughts!

Lastly, you're here in this world to "Learn and Love." School is never out for the pro, and the more love you give, the more you get! Make sure you give at least three hugs a day...especially if you love to receive hugs!

Shields: What advice would you give to someone who is just starting out but is fearful?

Davenport: Mind the gap! Success happens between your ears. Stop that stinkin' thinkin'! Believe that anything is possible, because it is! If you don't believe it is possible for you, borrow someone else's belief as your own. Know that there are people who believe in you and many have gone before you. Borrow their beliefs. Learn from their examples. I love to hum the famous song "Tin Man" by America. Remember when they say that the Wizard of Oz didn't give the Tin Man anything that he didn't already have? Remembering that always makes me smile when I have self-doubt about my ability to tackle a challenge.

Don't feel guilty by what you are giving up to go up. It is just a short-term exchange. It is worth it. As I built my career, many times I had to leave my boys as they were growing, but they gained more by watching me than if I would have given up my dreams. I'm convinced self-esteem is inherited. If you truly want your kids to succeed, then focus on making something out of yourself. From you, they will learn they can do anything they put their minds to if they want it bad enough. I was either going to give up working for forty hours for someone else for forty years or put in the time to build something for our family while making short-term sacrifices or working up front so later I could be totally present with them and have time and freedom long-term.

Shields: What does it mean to you to live your life alive?

Davenport: Living my life alive means waking up knowing that I followed what I was called to do. I even heard Dolly Parton say that recently when evaluating her amazing success! I identified with her message. Even when things were rough or didn't make sense, I followed that inner voice, which I always feel is the presence of God, and I decided to have fun with it! I never take myself too seriously, but I do take my life's mission to help others seriously.

Shields: What do you appreciate most about living your life alive?

Davenport: It means I can wake up knowing that I make a difference. I get to wake up and love people and encourage them to live their best lives. I get to be present with the people who are important to me. I go to bed at night satisfied with the choices I've made and live a life without regret. I always ask myself two questions before I go to sleep: what did I learn today, and what did I do today to help someone else?

To learn more about Rita Davenport, visit: www.RitaDavenport.com

Paul Dolman — Author, Speaker, Student, Teacher

Paul Dolman wrote the highly successful book *Hitchhiking with Larry David* (Gotham/Penguin), and his new book, *Martha's Vineyard Miracles*, is now available. He travels and gives talks on a variety of subjects.

He has been a professional musician, founded an entertainment company, and worked as a film producer in Hollywood. He currently divides his time between Martha's Vineyard and Anastasia Island.

Shields: What was it that "nudged" you to become an entrepreneur?

Dolman: I have always loved to create. For me, starting a business was an extension of my joy in creating something new and unique. Creating was also 100 times more interesting than simply plugging into a system that another person once found inspiring.

On top of that, I love the freedom of doing my own thing and writing my own rules. Controlling your time is essential to being happy and feeling a deep sense of fulfillment.

Shields: What wasn't working for you in your life that was holding you back from being the best you?

Dolman: There is natural inertia and primal fear that keeps us all from pushing out of our comfort zones into our edge. I was also a bit lazy and had created a nice degree of success with less than full effort. So for a long time, I just coasted and reaped the spoils of what I had. After a while, that began to feel toxic. Eventually, I simply made a choice to live at a higher level.

Shields: What is your single greatest success tip?

Dolman: There is no one magic thing, or even six. That said, I would say "deciding" to live in excellence and then taking action on a daily, consistent basis. Then falling in love with the process of the process. Celebrate all of it as a gift. Learn from both the wins and the near misses. Laugh at the pratfalls, and always have fun.

Shields: What advice would you give to someone who is just starting out but is fearful?

Dolman: My advice would be to dive in and begin. Getting started is the hardest part, so just start. It sounds simple and it is. Get a piece of paper and write your ideas down.... Then keep writing. You have started. Make a list of small goals, then larger ones. Again, have fun with it!

Shields: What does it mean to you to live your life alive?

Dolman: You open your eyes and you immediately feel a rush of inspiration because you love your life and the infinite possibilities of the day ahead. You are constantly in gratitude because you get to do the things you love while you never stop learning and meeting interesting people.

Life constantly amazes and surprises you with magic and miracles. You give more than you would ever take, as life continues to shower you with unimaginable abundance. You fall in love with life in a deeply romantic way, and this love blooms and grows like a wildfire.

At night, you fall asleep while counting your blessings.... Then you have sweet dreams of flying and dancing with angels.

Shields: What do you appreciate most about living your life alive?

Dolman: The absolute *miracle* of it all.... The fact that existence exists and I am this tiny particle in the fabric of Infinite Being...and have the ability to conceptualize a fraction of this truth.

To learn more about Paul Dolman, visit: www.PaulSamuelDolman.com

Donna Johnson — Author, Speaker, and Entrepreneur

Donna Johnson is the author of *Networking Today*. Her story has been featured in many books, including Chapter One of *Think & Grow Rich for Women* by Sharon Lechter. She is a co-author of *MLM Heart Attack: Restart the Heart and Your Dreams*. She was also the first consultant to reach the top level in her company. She shares her time with her husband between Wisconsin, Arizona, and Sweden.

Shields: What was it that "nudged" you to become an entrepreneur?

Johnson: I saw Network Marketing as an opportunity with no glass ceiling. I had no college degree and was a single mom of three small children with no child support. I loved the idea of truly putting my family first, and having a business that could revolve around my busy family life, not the other way around. I saw the value of true financial and time freedom.

Shields: What wasn't working for you in your life that was holding you back from being the best you?

Johnson: I really had to protect my focus and not "listen to the crowd" that was telling me to go get a "real job." I realized I was on the "road less traveled," and if I were going to reach my goals, I needed to put my blinders on and stay committed to my goals.

Shields: What is your single greatest success tip?

Johnson: I follow through and do what I say I'm going to do. I'm very efficient; I do the right things, and do enough of the right things long enough to achieve my goals. I'm diligent with my to-do lists and revenue-producing activities. I'm self-disciplined, so I don't need a "boss" to tell me to punch a clock.

Shields: What advice would you give to someone who is just starting out and is fearful?

Johnson: Jump "all in." Don't just say, "Oh, I'll give it a try." Make a commitment, share your goals with those who can help hold you accountable, and let them cheer you on. The world steps aside for the person who is clear on where she is going. Think Dorie in *Finding Nemo*.

Shields: What does it mean to you to live your life alive?

Johnson: It means to be always in touch with my TUG: The Ultimate Guide. It means to contribute and serve. I call it 3D Success: 1) Knowing what you do makes a difference, 2) Balance in your life, and 3) Financial Peace.

Shields: Out of all of the people who have influenced you, who was the biggest influence and why?

Johnson: My children. First, they were my "motivation" and "why" that fueled my drive. As they've grown, they've demonstrated to me that they benefited from living in a home where Mom was an entrepreneur, and they are now carrying on my legacy of "Living Life Alive."

Shields: What do you appreciate most about living your life alive?

Johnson: The example I set and the difference I can make to inspire others. If I had followed the crowd and gotten that "real job," I never would have been able to fund fully five orphanages around the world. I love waking up when I'm done sleeping, working when I want, traveling when I want, and living my life by design.

Shad Helmstetter — Best-Selling Author and International Speaker

Shad Helmstetter, Ph.D., is the international best-selling author of sixteen books in the field of personal growth, including *What to Say When You Talk to Your Self,* and *The Power of Neuroplasticity.* Dr. Helmstetter's books are published in many languages in over sixty-five countries.

Shields: What was it that "nudged" you to become an entrepreneur?

Helmstetter: Being an entrepreneur is really a personal attitude of being free, but with positive business goals and ideas in mind. I started life, very young, being taught by my father that there are no limits. For the best entrepreneurs, business and marketing ideas are just tools to use to promote winning ideas.

Shields: What wasn't working for you in your life that was holding you back from being the best you?

Helmstetter: I learned when I was very young that the only thing that can hold you back is "you." Fortunately, because

I had great programming from my parents early on, I never let that happen.

Shields: What is your single greatest success tip?

Helmstetter: You actually rewire your brain with the thoughts you think—especially the thoughts you repeat most often.

With what we now know about the brain's neuroplasticity—the ability of the brain to continue to change itself throughout our lives—we have learned that the ultimate key to success can be found in three words: repetition, repetition, repetition. The brain literally rewires itself with specific directions that are repeated. Repetition is the basis of all success.

Shields: What advice would you give to someone who is just starting out but is fearful?

Helmstetter: The simple answer is that most fear that we feel is actually caused by an overactive amygdala. That's a part of the brain that in ancient times alerted us when a saber-tooth tiger was about to attack. We no longer have saber-tooth tigers in our lives, but the amygdala part of our brain still thinks the tigers are after us. It's almost always a false alarm, but we stay on alert mentally, just in case.

The good news is that you can override the fear by practicing positive, repeated self-talk. Your positive self-talk will turn off the fear, when the fear was false in the first place.

Shields: What does it mean to you to live your life alive?

Helmstetter: Life can be like channel surfing through days and months, and getting nowhere. Or, if you're mindful and aware of who you are, why you're here, and what you're doing with your life each day, then life can be an amazingly wonderful opportunity to learn. Living your life alive gets down to being mindful of the smallest, wonderful details of the day.

Shields: Out of all of the people who influenced you, who has had the biggest effect and why?

Helmstetter: My father was one of my greatest influences. A brilliant man, he taught me to "throw the book away," and he taught me that if you look for it, you can always find a better way. That amazing concept taught me that whatever we think is the final answer today will almost always be overtaken by better, brighter ideas. Keep looking. You'll find them.

Shields: What do you appreciate most about living your life alive?

Helmstetter: Living your life alive makes you aware of everything around you. It slows things down, and it lets you appreciate what your life is really about. (It is not about mortgages, a job, and pleasing the boss.) A lot of people, most of them, miss life's real purpose almost entirely. People who live life alive practice being more aware. They live more, they find a deeper meaning in life, they live with a sense of purpose, and they're almost always happier.

To learn more about Shad Helmstetter, visit www.ShadHelmstetter.com.

Patrick Snow — International Best-Selling Author, Professional Keynote Speaker, Publishing and Marketing Publishing Coach, and Speaker Coach

Patrick Snow is the author of *Boy Entrepreneur*, *The Affluent Entrepreneur*, and *Creating Your Own Destiny*. Patrick hosts and leads Best Seller Publishing Institutes nationwide. He lives on Maui and travels internationally as an author, speaker, and coach.

Shields: What was it that "nudged" you to become an entrepreneur?

Snow: As a thirteen-year-old kid, I had a newspaper route and delivered the *Detroit Free Press* seven days a week from 5 to 7 a.m. Getting up was no fun, but I did this for a year, and then I learned that I could earn more money and work fewer hours (and sleep in) by selling *Detroit Free Press* subscriptions door-to-door. I would earn $2.00 when I sold a daily subscription, $1.00 when I sold a Sunday subscription, and $3.00 when I sold a Sunday and a daily. I would do this every Tuesday and Thursday evening from 6 to 9 p.m. I would often earn $80-100 per night cash on the spot. This was the amount I earned in a month delivering papers. I soon attached the concept of "selling" to "entrepreneurship" and never desired ever again to work for another person other than myself. It took a college degree and fifteen years' experience selling in corporate America before I could retire from my job at thirty-five years old and go full-time into my business as an author, professional speaker, and publishing coach. Now, ten years later, I have so enjoyed the financial benefits of being an entrepreneur and the time freedom that this lifestyle has given to me. More importantly, it has virtually allowed me single-handedly to raise my two boys, coach all of their sports teams, and be there for them as a father. This was priceless and only could have been achieved through the choice of becoming an entrepreneur.

Shields: What wasn't working for you in your life that was holding you back from being the best you?

Snow: What has never worked for me is having a boss who has less experience, less qualifications, and less knowledge telling me what to do, how to sell, how to market, how to close the accounts when he/she doesn't even know that client's needs, buyers, concerns, or details. I have never been one to be "bossed around." However, whenever I have been able to find a mentor whom I trust and respect (and some of these have been my bosses), I would have gone to the end of the world for them and done whatever they asked. I always tried to glean as much knowledge, skills, and strategy as I could from those I respected. Furthermore, having a glass ceiling, as did a capped income, has also held me back. I believe as an entrepreneur, you should be compensated based on the amount of value that you bring to the marketplace.

Shields: What is your single greatest success tip?

Snow: My greatest success tip is to soul search for your innermost marketable passions and then transform your innermost marketable passions into your profession by becoming a business owner. Once you start your business, then you need to focus 50 percent of your efforts on prospecting and developing trust and respect with your buyers; finally, ask for the sale, and then under-promise and over-deliver. Also, note that successful businesses take three times longer than we anticipate and cost three times more than we budget. Therefore, the key to succeed in business is to survive the 3X the time and 3X the money (during the janitor years) so you can get to the 30X your day job income as a result of benefiting for a lifetime (during the CEO years).

Shields: What advice would you give to someone who is just starting out but is fearful?

Snow: My best advice is to keep your day job as long as you can and double dip with multiple streams of income. By doing so, it will minimize the anxiety, build your confidence, and then also remove much of the risk. With this extra income, do all you can to become debt-free from a consumer loan standpoint and have one year's worth of income saved in the bank. Once you find yourself in this position and your business income has surpassed your day job income (and you're passionate about your business), then I give my blessing for that someone to go full-time in his or her business.

Shields: What does it mean to you to live your life alive?

Snow: It means that I live my life on my terms, my time, my schedule, and my passions. It means to have the freedom and flexibility to travel when I want and stay home when I want. It means having a choice to work your passions, or do nothing at all. It means not having someone (an employer) always looking over your shoulder, pulling your strings like a puppet. It simply means to me having more time, more money, more freedom, more peace, more love, and more happiness in life. It means living your passions daily, focusing on your health and wellness, not worrying about money, serving others, and creatively bringing more value to the marketplace as an entrepreneur. It means being active, but every now and again slowing down to smell the flowers and count our many blessing in life.

Shields: Out of all of the people who influenced you, who was the biggest influence and why?

Snow: There are so many people who have influenced me over the years, but one who immediately pops out was one of my youth sports coaches, Bill McCarrick, who pushed me further than what I thought was possible. But the person who influenced me the most was my father, Jack Snow.

As I look back on my life, I realize he always believed in me, never judged me, and always encouraged me to "live my life alive." He may be the only person who has ever understood me and how and why I think and act the way that he does. Before his passing after a yearlong fight with cancer, I wrote him a six-page love letter thanking him for all the ways he had impacted my life. I counted fourteen major ways that immediately stuck out, but there are probably another 100 or so. I have learned from him that the greatest gift parents can give their children is "belief" in them...their dreams, goals, and visions. He always believed in me no matter how lofty my goals were. In one of my last conversations with him, I thanked him for being the best dad a kid could ask for, and I thanked him for always believing in me. I will never forget his response as he said: "Patrick, you were always very determined, so you made it easy for me to believe in you!" He taught me that I could achieve any dream, goal, or vision as long as I worked for it and paid for it myself. In my heart, he is and was the single greatest man who has walked on this earth and will always have a profound impact on me as an entrepreneur, father, and member of planet earth.

Shields: What do you appreciate most about living your life alive?

Snow: FREEDOM! There is no question about it. Living my life alive has given me time freedom, money freedom, and creative freedom to do what I want, when I want, where I want, and with whom I want. With this freedom also comes responsibility, and for that reason, it is important for us as successful entrepreneurs that we constantly give back and help others in need. We need to help as many employees as we can break the mode of dependence and help them succeed as entrepreneurs so they can, in turn, serve others as well. I love the freedom I have being an author, professional speaker, and publishing coach, and this is what I most enjoy about living my passions. If I can be of service or help you in any way, please feel free to reach out to me.

To learn more about Patrick Snow, visit www.PatrickSnow.com

Christy Dreiling — Entrepreneur, Producer, Author, Model, and Actress

Christy Dreiling lives in Kansas with her husband and three boys. She has studied failure and success. Although Dreiling was raised poor, she has chosen a life of success and has opened her heart to pour out love to others. Regardless of the professional hat she is wearing, it is obvious love resides there. Dreiling is the author of *LOL—From Homeless to Multimillion-Dollar Global Business Leader* and her children's book, *Holes in My Socks*.

> **Shields:** What was it that "nudged" you to become an entrepreneur?

> **Dreiling:** There was no "one" thing that nudged me. It was as though my soul knew that entrepreneurship would be my destiny. I was shy of the confidence to believe that I

could be an entrepreneur. Watching my mother be abused, and being abused myself along with my sisters, created a hunger and a curiosity that led me to question if the "traditional" ways that we all were taught in school and in our home were indeed meant for all. I believe we are all souls meant to live freely and express our divine essence and gifts that we've brought into this world. Becoming an entrepreneur has been a process of loving myself enough to be willing enough to openly and authentically share that which I know to help others expand and grow in their life missions here.

Shields: What wasn't working for you in your life that was holding you back from being the best you?

Dreiling: There are still desires of the heart, and I am not there yet. But I no longer try to judge that. I accept how I am feeling and I pay attention. If I am not pleased, it's because I have been distracted or resistant to change. Fear is usually to blame. Confidence is always a close second. But a lack of confidence comes from the fear of lack of love. If we proceed and embrace a new journey, we are taught that it's bad to fail. That only those who have perfect attendance, perfect grades, perfect families or careers are the accomplished ones. This is not true and so far off course. This is why we see so much dysfunction and unhappiness. What is not taught is that there is nothing to fear because it is necessary for our growth here to fail forward and to jump up and to go again. Most people who fail stay down because they are afraid. They are afraid of being judged or not loved. There is always a better version of me that I seek. I work on her daily, but I embrace her daily as well. And I stomp on that voice that tries to beat her up. I'm doing the best I can now with the tools I have. Can't wait to see how far I go.

Shields: What is your single greatest success tip?

Dreiling: It's important to be hungry, but even more important to stay humble and hungry. When good fortune chases you, say thank you and keep doing good deeds, but do not require it for your own personal joy.

Shields: What advice would you give to someone who is just starting out but is fearful?

Dreiling: My advice is that you have already taken this journey before! "How?" you ask. Remember when you wanted to learn how to ride a bike, swim, read, drive, or be a parent? Remember the fear of failing or falling? But what caused you to want to master it? You believed it would bring more into your life. It was something new and exciting. You have already been down this road you have just forgotten. Remember, though, that after a while, the fear wore off and the newness wore off. You must realize that in order to become better at whatever it is you wish, you have to invest time and energy into it. If you stop because you get fearful, you have walked out on your very best "you," wishing to expand itself. Fear is just an illusion unless you are being chased by a hungry lion; then you better run and run fast! But everything else that you cannot see, touch, or feel that you think could hurt you is just your ego afraid of change.

Shields: What does it mean to you to live your life alive?

Dreiling: To truly desire growth! To crave learning and sharing and, of course, expanding love. Loving others but also deeply loving and accepting oneself for all that you are and all that you have come here to be.

Shields: Out of all of the people who influenced you, who was the biggest influence and why?

Dreiling: This I cannot honestly answer. There are hundreds of thousands who have made up the tapestry of the evolution of my soul. Each person, animal, and experience has been a great teacher for me.

Shields: What do you appreciate most about living your life alive?

Dreiling: That I know with all of my heart and soul that nothing that happens to us is ever by accident. Initially good or not, good happens from it because we must learn before we expand to our next level of higher consciousness. Love *right* where you are and also equally important is to *love* where others are no matter where they are. Allow them to have their time to learn and grow here. Please don't judge them; they already do enough of that themselves. Embrace and accept that they too are here to grow and become their best version, and if we all just patted one another a little bit more and said, "You got this! Don't worry; you'll make it," then think, where would our world be? Where could it be?

Dr. Dennis Banks — Psychiatrist

Dr. Banks is a psychiatrist in Wailea, Hawaii. He received his medical degree from Yale University School of Medicine and has been in practice for over twenty years. Dr. Banks also has a law degree and was a Visiting Scholar in Law and Psychiatry at Harvard Law school.

> **Shields:** As a psychiatrist, what do you think living your life alive actually means?

> **Banks:** Psychiatry is an area of specialty in the medical field. It is my job as a doctor to diagnosis and treat serious psychiatric illnesses but also to give people with lesser afflictions the tools to improve their lives and circumstances.

> Personally, I believe living your life alive means doing what you like to do. It is being able to construct my life in a way that I can bring together interests and passions that are fundamental to whom I am. This could, for others, be an epiphany or a gradual process. Personally, I navigated through the puzzle by choosing pieces that fit what I wanted in life. One of my desires was to expand my practice to Maui. Maui had so many things to offer that wooed my interests and passions. If I lacked specific pieces, it wouldn't

have happened. If you are lacking pieces of the puzzle, then it won't happen, and that is why is it so important to know what pieces you need to pick up.

Living your life alive does not mean you have to walk around in this excited state constantly, but maybe even more importantly, it means you settle into peace and contentment.

Shields: Could you share some characteristics or behaviors of people whom you believe live their lives alive?

Banks: People who display happiness and joy are usually living their lives alive, and many times, it is because they are doing something that they believe is important. Many times, they are people who had first dreamt something and then are actually living their dreams. People who assemble their lives in such a way of putting their passions with their work are happier. For example, if someone loves horses and can find work or a business that deals with horses, that person will feel more fulfilled in life.

Shields: What do you believe holds people back from living their lives alive?

Banks: Chance, opportunity, and people imprison themselves with relationships or jobs that hold them back. They believe they have insufficiencies of some kind or another. People can also be lazy. Living your life alive is work. It doesn't come passively. This is a hard course to take, and not everyone will. It takes determination. People also, many times, let distractions play a larger role than the things they are trying to accomplish.

People also let fear stop them. Fear from a psychiatry point of view translates into anxiety. There are actual fears, such as arachnophobia, but what most people consider fear is actually anxiety that most likely developed early by learning how we act life out. How we are modeled or treated can form a foundation of how we handle anxiety about different situations. I would encourage people to put their lives together and gather what is needed to make it happen. It can be done.

Shields: What suggestions or tools would you suggest to people who don't feel like they are living their best lives?

Banks: Be modest and humble. Have appreciation for the simple things you may take for granted, such as the shelter you have or the plate of food you are about to eat. Set realistic goals for yourself. You are in a position right now. Be real about it and then work on setting yourself up for what you want. If you want to climb Mt. Everest, that is great, but you probably can't do it tomorrow. What steps do you need to take to get there?

Don't focus on money. Focus on doing what you like to do. The most successful way to have money is to be generous.

Shields: Who or what was the biggest influence in modeling or assisting you in living your life alive?

Banks: I have had many teachers who helped me find my own path and walk it out. The lama I studied under, in New York, was a perfect example of honesty, compassion, and integrity. The book *The Diamond Cutter* has been a great influence in my life and how I view success and business. Money cannot bring happiness, but gratitude can.

At the end of the day, feeling content is living my life alive.

To learn more about Dr. Dennis Banks, visit: www.DrDennis-Banks.com

Ashley Castle — Global Entrepreneur and Multimedia Travel Journalist

Ashley Castle works with brands such as Travelocity, MINI Cooper, Leading Hotels of the World, and Wyndham to help them tell their unique stories. You'll find her scuba diving in Bonaire or rafting down a river in Panama. She's created her dream life, and her mission and passion is helping other people to do the same. Here she tells her story of living her life alive in her own words.

I stumbled into being an entrepreneur. It all started with feelings of dissatisfaction. I was twenty-three years old, recently out of college, and in my first job. It only took me a few months in my new position to start asking the question, "Is this really all there is?" I realized quickly that I didn't want to wake up every morning and go to work for someone else, be told when I could take off, and when I could take a vacation, and, in addition to all of this, live paycheck to paycheck. A burning desire for more was in my heart, but I had no idea how to get it.

A few months later, I was introduced to a network marketing business. I had never done anything in sales and didn't think I was qualified for the job, but this seemed to be my best option to have what I wanted to have in life, so I jumped in with both feet. I actually dove in headfirst! Within a year and a half, I reached my company's top level of management and was its youngest person at that level in the company's twenty-five-plus-year history.

Although I was experiencing a lot of success, I had a lot of personal growth to do in order to become the person I am now. I had some big personal struggles, and I invested a lot of time to work on myself. I spent nearly two months traveling through India back in 2009, and although I had done some international traveling before, that trip transformed my life. It birthed the desire not only to have abundance, but to make a bigger contribution in the world. I moved to New York City a year later and continued developing myself and pursuing my dreams. All of these things were possible because I had said "Yes" a few years prior to becoming an entrepreneur and creating a residual income.

I have created my dream life: I am a multi-media travel journalist, in addition to running my global health and wellness company. I make a living from traveling the world, but more than that, each day I wake up and create my life. My personal goal in all that I do is to inspire people to wake up and realize that life is incredibly short! We all have things we want to do, places we want to see, and people we want to become. It's time to get rid of your "someday" and start living out your desires now. No one else can do that but you, which is what "living your life alive" is all about.

For more information about Ashley Castle, reach out to her at:
Instagram: @itsashleycastle
Twitter: @itsashleycastle

A FINAL NOTE

"This year I choose to live beyond my wildest dreams.
I wonder where that will take me?"

— Oprah

As we come to the end of this book, it's time to ask yourself: What am I going to do about living my life alive?" What have you already done to live your life alive?

Remember the Marianne Williamson quote from earlier in the book? It's a powerful enough message that I want to repeat it here:

"Our deepest fear is not that we are inadequate. Our deepest fear is that we are powerful beyond measure. It is our light, not our darkness that most frightens us. We ask ourselves, who am I to be brilliant, gorgeous, talented, and fabulous? Actually, who are you not to be? You are a child of God. Your playing small does not serve the world. There is nothing enlightened about shrinking so that other people will not feel insecure around you. We are all meant to shine, as children do. We were born to make manifest the glory of God that is within us. It is not

just in some of us; it is in everyone and as we let our own light shine, we unconsciously give others permission to do the same. As we are liberated from our own fear, our presence automatically liberates others."

— Marianne Williamson

I challenge you to continue on this journey and take action steps to live your life alive like never before.

In this final exercise, list the ten things you are going to commit to doing in the next ninety days to make sure that living your life alive happens or continues to happen for you:

1. _____

2. _____

3. _____

4. _____

5. _____

6. _____

7. _____

8. _____

9. _____

10. _____

In this book, you learned not only to dream again, but to live your life authentically and alive. You learned that no matter what is in your way, you can overcome it, and you are not alone. You have done some self-reflection and discovery, and now you have the tools to put your vision into action. Why not you?

Now that you have finished this book, I would like to continue to stay in touch. Please contact me and let me know what you liked/ disliked about the book so I can release an even better version for my future friends (readers). Tell me about your challenges and what you learned.

I would like to offer you a way to stay in touch and a complimentary life or business coaching session, with no obligation, by phone or Skype.

Here is my private contact info:

www.LivingYourLifeAlive.com
LivingYourLifeAlive@gmail.com
autumn.envp@gmail.com
Skype: Autumn Shields

Also, please Like the book on Facebook: Living Your Life Alive

Thank you for reading this book. I wish you the best and know you will live your life alive!

ABOUT THE AUTHOR

Autumn Shields is an international speaker, author, coach, and entrepreneur. She has one son whom she had the pleasure of guiding from birth into adulthood. She grew up in Colorado and now lives on the beautiful island of Maui, Hawaii. After learning to listen to her inner voice and feeling the nudge, she built a successful business through network marketing. Before she started her own business, she was in law enforcement for over fifteen years. She was a Victim Advocate Director for police departments, helping crime victims. She did crisis intervention counseling, community referrals, and court support. She also did probation work with offenders and volunteered in a women's prison. On Maui, she has developed a project for a non-profit that helps high-risk teens find their strengths through a curriculum of self-discovery. Her passion is to help others overcome their obstacles, find their true passions, and live their lives alive.

ABOUT NETWORK MARKETING

Network marketing is where ordinary people can choose to live an extraordinary life.

Network marketing is a type of business opportunity that is very popular with people looking for part-time, flexible businesses. Some of the best-known companies fall under the network-marketing umbrella.

There are many misconceptions about network marketing, and not all companies are created equal. However, network marketing is not a pyramid scheme. Pyramid schemes are illegal. If there is some big, upfront investment or no products are being moved and the only goal is enrolling people, it is most likely illegal.

How does network marketing really work? It is simply a distribution system. See the following chart.

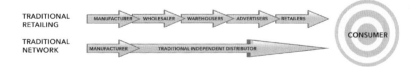

- Marketing and distributing a product via word of mouth
- Flexible schedule
- Ownership opportunity
- Effective distribution system
- Company provides infrastructure
- Lifestyle choices

So, let's say you buy a shirt for $40.00 at a retail store. I am sure you have done this before. You are used to paying that even though you know the shirt probably cost $3.00 to make. You understand why you pay more. You have to pay for the shirt to be made, transported, sold to the wholesaler, stored, transported to the retailer, then advertised, plus to pay for the retailer's retail space and utilities and the cost of hiring retail employees to sell you the shirt. Every time the product changes hands, it costs about 20 percent more. We all would like to buy direct and skip all of the "middle men." If you needed to get the floors in your house redone and I told you my uncle could get the materials direct from the suppliers, you would be thrilled you got the hookup and saved money on a good quality product! Or what if I told you I have a friend who can get you the car you want straight from the manufacturer and you don't have to get it from the dealership? That would be awesome, wouldn't it? That is the basic way network marketing works. In fact, that is how I got involved. If someone asked me to start any kind of business thirteen years ago, especially a network marketing business, I would have run the other way. I had no business being in business! I was working fifty-plus hours a week, on-call 24/7, helping raise four children at home, and volunteering on a board to open a house for teenage moms. I didn't have time to think, let alone start a business. In addition, the last thing I sold was Girl Scout cookies, and that was in the second grade. I actually was pretty good at that gig. Perhaps it was just a loved product. To top it off, I was a professional for goodness sake. I thought, "Only those cute moms who want to stay home with their children and make a few hundred dollars a month do these types of businesses." Wow! Nothing like being very uneducated and unaware of an industry and making judgments that I knew nothing about.

Upfront, I never decided to "do" this type of business. I started using the products and saw results. I joined for the discounts and to be able to shop for myself so I could reap the benefits. I started telling my friends about the products and the discounts they could receive. I never realized that was "how" the business worked. Believe it or not, I got a small paycheck and called my company. I told it, "Don't send checks; I'm not doing this business." Can you imagine the person who took that call? She must have thought, "Wow, I have a real bright one on the phone." She kindly responded to me, "Well, when you refer the products to others, we pay you." I paused and thought about it for two seconds and replied, "Oh! Game on! I can do that! I love this stuff!"

We all naturally refer people to things we like or believe in. I send people to restaurants I like all the time. I also review the restaurants online, which helps their businesses grow. They don't even give me a free meal, but in network marketing, we get compensated for sharing. So how are these network-marketing companies able to pay for many people to make a really good income and not just a few like in many corporations? And how do they hand out trips and sometimes cars to hundreds, if not thousands, of people a year? Think about that for a minute. It's because they choose to pay people for spreading the word instead of pouring millions into the traditional way of getting a product to you and paying a celebrity millions to say he uses the product when we know most of them don't, and we don't think that is somehow a scam? Also, companies can keep the money they are not spending in the traditional retail method and put it toward product development that can keep the products evolving.

Network marketing is word-of-mouth marketing. Obviously, with technology, it has grown to being shared in many different ways, but it is still one person sharing what he or she believes in with others.

We have learned to search and price compare online, and now online shopping has surpassed retail sales. We love this because of convenience and because we believe we have shopped around and received the best deal.

However, receiving products through the system of network marketing is either helping you save money or grow a business. If you are not directly involved with the company, you are supporting the person who introduced you and others in the company. Consumers are becoming smarter about not only the quality and safety of the products they are purchasing but whom their money is ultimately supporting.

Network marketing programs feature a low upfront investment—usually only a few hundred dollars for the purchase of a product sample kit—and the opportunity to sell a product line as well as teach and train others to do the same.

I hear many different objections or concerns about this industry, and I could fill pages by listing them all, but I would rather break it down and show you how I see it. If it sounds too good to be true, it probably is. Network marketing is "work." That is why it is called Net "work" marketing. It is not sit on the couch, think thoughts, and get rich.

Network marketing is a rectangle:

> Everyone starts at the bottom. You don't get a place in the organization by your resume, years of experience, the initials (or lack of them) behind your name, or whether there is a position open for you. You start at the bottom. Just like everyone else. It is an even playing field! It is where ordinary people can live extraordinary lives—if they choose and work at it! There is a lot of room at the top! Depending on your efforts and commitment, you get to decide to move up in the organization and increase your pay at your pace. Yes! You decide. You are CEO of your own business.

Most companies or government agencies are triangles aka pyramids:

You apply and get accepted into a position...(if available) depending on your skills, experience, education/degrees, and whom you know. You can only move up if a position opens up and you are qualified to move up and make more money. You are usually working forty-plus hours a week with a few weeks for vacation or sick time. Only a few people will ever end up at the top.

Why are so many people joining the triangle? The trend today says people want to work for themselves and create wealth while having flexibility. They want their work to revolve around their lives and not their lives revolve around their work. Isn't that what you want?

If so, then you are welcome to reach out to me or explore what company would be a good fit for you.

ABOUT THE MAKOA PROJECT

The Makoa Project was envisioned in early 2013. I thought that if I started a program anywhere, it would be serving girls in Thailand to help them break free from the sex trade, but in January 2013, I was nudged to serve on Maui. I thought, "What would the needs be on Maui? Are there needs?"

Although many know Maui as paradise, and it is in many ways, there is a huge need for local children and teens. Hawaii is the worst state to make income in, and it is ranked fiftieth out of fifty in education. The average income for individuals in Hawaii is $29,500, yet the cost-of-living is approximately 30 percent higher than the mainland. An average home sells for $530,000 or rents for $2,500 per month. In many families, both parents have two or three jobs each. There are limited resources and limited opportunities for families to prosper. Many families are not even able to travel off the island due to travel costs.

The Makoa Project is a discovery program for *na keiki* (children) and teens to learn, through an innovative approach, about their authentic selves and to equip them to help discover and live out their true passions. Most of the youth whom The Makoa Project works with are abusing or have abused some sort of drug. Cocaine and meth are a big threat to the youth on Maui. By equipping the youth with tools and visions for their own lives, the cultural, economic, and community development overall will be improved. By partnering with existing agencies such as Maui Youth and Family Services, The Makoa Project connects with children and teens to focus on empowerment, growth, and understanding of self...all while having fun!

The Makoa is funded 100 percent by donations. All Makoa Project staff are volunteers. All funds go to direct services!

Please consider donating and helping the *na keiki* of Maui build a bigger vision for their lives.

Go to: http://www.myfs.org/
Click on: How to Help and Donate Now
Designate funds to The Makoa Project

Thank you in advance for making a difference! Your support is important!

BOOK AUTUMN SHIELDS
TO SPEAK AT YOUR NEXT EVENT

When it comes to choosing a passionate speaker for your next event, you'll find no one more capable of transforming your audience than Autumn. She will lead you and your group on a transformational journey. Her stories and experiences are both inspiring as well as comical. By taking just a small step with Autumn, you will overcome fear, learn how to live your life alive, and see amazing things happen.

Whether your audience is 10 or 10,000, in North America or abroad, Autumn Shields will deliver a tailored message for your meeting, conference, or classroom. Speaking topics include:

- Leading from within
- Living your passion out loud
- Doing what matters
- Overcoming fears, obstacles, or trauma

- Embracing abundance
- Having faith
- Defining self
- Healthy living
- Finding your authentic self

To arrange for Autumn to come speak to your group or organization, contact her at:

www.LivingYourLifeAlive.com
LivingYourLifeAlive@gmail.com